The Amazing
TOMATO
COOKBOOK

Photography: Lewis Morley
Cover Photography: John Macmichael
Cookery Editor: Elizabeth Carden
Recipe Testing: Karen Davidson

Published by Bay Books Pty Ltd
61–69 Anzac Parade,
KENSINGTON • NSW 2033

© Bay Books

Publisher: George Barber
National Library of Australia
Card Number and ISBN 1 86256 010 2

The publisher wishes to thank the following for
their generous assistance during the photography of
this book: Peters of Kenzington, Anzac Parade,
Kensington, NSW; Saywell Imports, 20–30 Maddox
St, Alexandria, NSW

BB86

The Amazing
TOMATO
COOKBOOK

Mary-Lou Arnold   Jane Aspinwall   Douglas Marsland

Duske Teape-Davis   Jan Wunderlich

BAY BOOKS
SYDNEY AND LONDON

CONTENTS

ato Melange • Braised Zucchini and Tomatoes • Ratatouille • Arabian Mixed Vegetables • Beans Provencale • Italian Vegetable Hot Pot • Scalloped Potatoes and Tomatoes • Tomato and Chick Pea Subji • Cauliflower Koftas in Tomato Sauce • Prawn and Egg Curry • Crab and Prawn Creole • Nutmeat Ratatouille • Chicken Liver Snack

Tomatoes with their glorious colour, tantalising aroma and distinctive flavour are one of the welcome signs that summer has arrived. In fact, we've become such dedicated fans of the tomato that, thanks to commercial hot-houses, it is available all year round. But nothing is more flavoursome than those allowed to ripen naturally, in the sunshine.

More popular even than the fresh fruit — judging by sales figures — are the numerous prepacked alternatives on the market — canned or pureed tomatoes, tomato paste, or freeze-dried flakes or those turned into ketchup, sauces, chutneys and relishes; the range increases all the time as manufacturers develop imaginative new presentation methods for our favourite culinary asset.

Tomatoes are a popular ingredient in the recipes of almost every culture, though they became so only by accident. Because they belong to the same plant family as deadly nightshade, tomatoes were initially dogged with an unfair reputation for being poisonous. In fact, they are rich in vital vitamins and also refreshingly low in kilojoules. Unlike most fruit and vegetables, they lose few nutrients in cooking.

The tomato seems to have been first used in cookery when Mexican Aztec Indians, curious about the weed that thrived among their maize crops, sampled the fruit and found not only that it was safe to eat but also a welcome sharp addition to their otherwise bland dishes. It swiftly became a staple and since then has formed the basis of many recipes — such as chilli or tortilla (omelette) — that we today associate with Central and South American cuisine.

The tomato was borne back to Europe from Mexico by the gold-seeking Spanish conquistadores, who prized the decorative qualities of the original yellow-coloured fruit. When introduced to the Spanish-ruled kingdom of Naples, in Italy, it was christened 'pomo d'oro' — golden apple.

The newly-imported fruit thrived in the sunny Mediterranean climate and was soon cheaply and popularly available to all, with the result that adventurous cooks in both countries developed their own range of tomato-based recipes from soups, like the famous Spanish Gazpacho or the country's particular style of omelette, casserole, meat dishes like Veal Parmigiana or the doughey Pissaladiere. The tomato's very individual flavour was soon recognised as ideal to enhance dishes based on meat, poultry, fish, cheese, eggs, rice, pasta and vegetables and, as enthusiasm for its versatility spread, other cultures contributed their own variations on the theme.

The French, who wrongly convinced themselves of its aphrodisiac qualities, dubbed the tomato the 'pomme d'amour' — the love apple, but overcame their suspicions when Napoleon's Spanish wife Empress Eugenie introduced tomato-based recipes to the court, and they eventually went on to provide some of the most famous dishes of all, such as Ratatouille and Tomates a la Provencale.

Pissaladiere

Veal Parmigiana

Gazpacho

Types of Tomatoes

The universal popularity which prompted its cultivation in every country and climate led to the development of many different types of tomato, three of which are now widely sold:
Common salad tomatoes: Best eaten raw, these tomatoes have a good bright red colour with firm, but not hard flesh.
Cherry or Tom Thumbs: These are the very tiny tomatoes which are excellent scattered in a salad, used in creating interesting hors d'oeuvres, or turned into a garnish.
Roma or plum tomatoes: These are ideal for cooking and are best when slightly soft and past their prime. The flavour intensifies when heated and the Roma makes an excellent basis for a sauce or puree as it has denser flesh and less juice than other varieties. These are most commonly cultivated for canning and may easily be poured in to form the basis of a tasty casserole.

Common Salad Tomatoes

Cherry Tomatoes or Tom Thumbs

Buying tomatoes

Good quality tomatoes should be plump and firm, heavy in the hand and faintly aromatic. If possible, select ones which still have the stem attached as they will retain their moisture and remain fresh longer. Avoid tomatoes that are bruised, split, grossly misshapen or unevenly coloured; the latter means they have been chilled or exposed to too high a heat and will have a poor flavour and ripen badly. Poor quality tomatoes have usually been picked prematurely while very green and then ripened at a temperature that was either too low or high.

As a rule it's better to buy tomatoes as you need them — firm and ripe for salads, soft but unbruised for soups, purees and casseroles — rather than storing the fruit for long periods.

Ripening and storage

Tomatoes are always best eaten as fresh as possible, but it is possible to ripen the fruit after purchase — after all, most of the tomatoes we buy have been picked when green and allowed to ripen en route to the shops, or by artificial processes.

If you want to use tomatoes in a few days time, it is best to buy ones that are pale green, with just a hint of pink around the calyx, or light red in colour. They can be ripened at home in a paper bag or cupboard, but it is important that they be kept out of direct light. If, for instance, they are placed on a sunny windowsill it's likely that they will colour up and flavour unevenly. Always remove any plastic wrapping and store ripened tomatoes in a cool dark place — remember that they gradually lose flavour when refrigerated, so this should be kept to a minimum. For best results, stand tomatoes at room temperature for an hour before eating.

Tomatoes which have been picked too young will not ripen and are best used in chutneys, pickles and relishes. It is possible to freeze tomatoes successfully for up to a year, but they should be medium to small in size and in peak condition.

Ripening Tomatoes

TOMATO TECHNIQUES

Peeling: The wide availability of ready-peeled, low-cost canned tomatoes makes this an unnecessary exercise when preparing a simple casserole or soup, but there are some recipes for which freshly-peeled tomatoes are invaluable.

To peel a ripe fruit, cut out the core with a small, sharp knife and score the other end with a cross. Put the tomatoes in a bowl and pour boiling water over them, leaving them to soak for 10 seconds or until the skin starts peeling back. Remove, strip the skin, then cut out the blossom at the stem end with a knife.

Seeding tomatoes: It is very simple to remove the seeds from tomatoes and the little time and effort it takes will be amply rewarded in your cooking. The little seeds in tomatoes can spoil the appearance and texture of some recipes and, when cooked, may impart a slightly bitter taste to a delicately flavoured dish. All you do is cut the tomato in half, crosswise, and gently squeeze each half over a sieve. Scoop out any remaining seeds with a teaspoon. Discard the seeds and reserve the liquid to use in your cooking.

1 Using a small sharp knife, cut out the core

2 Score the other end of the tomato with a cross

3 Place the tomatoes in a glass bowl and cover with boiling water

4 Peel away and discard the skin

Seeding a tomato

Making tomato pulp or concentrate

Peeled and seeded tomatoes can be cooked into a versatile pulp which can be sieved to make a soup or sauce, added to thicken a casserole or gently reduced to a thick concentrate. Concentrated tomato paste is the best way to freeze tomatoes as it takes up minimum space and can be reused by diluting it with a little stock, water or wine to the desired consistency.

The pulp or concentrate can be frozen in small containers or icecube trays and then removed and stored in a plastic bag. This will keep for a year unless the tomatoes were very ripe when cooked. In this case it is best to keep the pulp frozen for no more than one month.

Cooking and freezing tomato pulp

Garnishing Techniques

Its rich colour and versatility make the tomato an ideal candidate for garnish, and here some favourite tomato decorations.

Vandyking tomatoes: Using a sharp knife, cut through the centre of the tomato in a zigzag fashion and carefully divide in two when the fruit has been cut all the way round.

1 Using a sharp knife cut through to the centre of the tomato in a zigzag fashion

2 When the tomato has been cut all the way around divide into two halves

Tomato rose: With a small sharp knife, cut a slice from the base of a firm tomato and continue peeling the fruit in a spiral, taking care not to break the skin. Place the peel on a board and loosely wind it to form a neat roll like the base of a rose and secure with a toothpick. Wind a second piece of skin tightly to form the rose's centre, place it in the middle and secure with a toothpick.

1 Continue peeling the tomato in a spiral without breaking the skin

2 Forming the tomato rose

Tomato tulip: Making six diagonal cuts, slice halfway down the tomato and peel the skin back with a small sharp knife, taking care not to cut it too finely as the peel will dry out. The tomato tulip provides an attractive garnish for salads, seafood platters and glazed legs of ham.

1 Make six diagonal cuts across the tomato cutting down half way

2 With a small sharp knife peel back the skin. Do not cut too finely or the skin will dry out

Herbs, spices and flavourings

Although the tomato needs no more than a touch of salt, pepper and sugar to bring out its incomparable sweet and sour flavouring, every culture has its favourite additions, whether serving the fruit raw or cooked. Fresh herbs like basil, oregano, tarragon, chives, sage, dill and parsley all subtly enhance its personality and provide an interesting visual contrast with their differing shapes and colour. Chilli, capers, ginger, curry and mustard also make flavoursome and sometimes piquant additions. Garlic is a natural accompaniment to tomato as are olive oil, cream, yoghurt and cheese, which add texture as well as flavour.

Onion is the vegetable that crops up most commonly in tomato recipes but the type used as an ingredient in many of the dishes featured is the cause of some confusion. For depending on where you live, it goes by different names — in Australia, it's known as the shallot, while the British name is spring onion and exactly the same thing is called the shallot by Americans. But whatever you choose to call this tasty little onion, the flavour is the same worldwide!

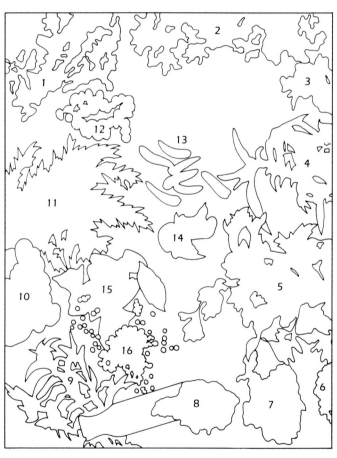

1 Watercress 2 Marjoram 3 Mint 4 Sage 5 Continental parsley 6 Parsley 7 Curry powder 8 Chilli powder 9 Tarragon 10 Ginger root 11 Dill 12 Capers 13 Chillies 14 Garlic 15 Bay leaves 16 Black peppercorns

Herbs and spices

SOUPS AND STARTERS

The warming colour of tomato soup can be every bit as enticing
as its flavour.
Choose tomatoes that have reached their prime — brilliant red
colour, sweet aroma, slightly soft to the touch. This will ensure
a soup that is full-flavoured and a rich red.
Not all soups are served hot. The Gazpacho, for example, is
served chilled, perfect for summer meals. But when the days slip
into winter, the rich Minestrone becomes a meal in itself, and
needs only to be served steaming hot, with crusty rolls.
Tomatoes lend themselves to the first course very well, not only
because they are a light, tasty start to a meal, but because they
have great visual appeal and, with a little garnishing, can add an
attractive finishing touch to any dish. The tomato is refreshing to
the palate and light on the digestive system, so it will not mar the
main course.
These days, tomatoes are available all year round, and they can
be served in any season. For example, a chilled soup is ideal for
summer, and Gnocchi with Tomato Sauce is a delicious winter
starter.

Crumbed Sardines with Tomato Coulis

Tomato Soup

4 large tomatoes
2 cups water
pinch bicarbonate of soda
1 cup milk
1 tablespoon flour blended
 with 20 g softened butter
salt and cayenne pepper

Boil the tomatoes in the water until soft, add soda, then rub through a sieve. Return the mixture to a clean saucepan, add milk, butter and blended flour, and season to taste with salt and cayenne pepper. Serve piping hot.

Serves 4

Tomato Consomme

This recipe requires a little time and concentration but is a classical cookery method, well worth the effort. Adding the egg whites to the stock will collect impurities leaving the liquid sparkling clear.

1.5 litres chicken or beef
 stock
8 large tomatoes, cored,
 peeled and chopped
1 bacon bone
1 teaspoon lemon juice
dash tarragon vinegar
eggs
white wine as required
freshly ground black pepper

Put the stock, tomatoes, bacon bone, lemon juice and vinegar into a large saucepan and bring to the boil. Simmer for 1 hour then strain and cool. Refrigerate to allow the fat to set on top.

Remove the fat and measure the soup. For every 2 cups of soup use the shells and whites of 3 eggs and ¼ cup white wine and bring to the boil, whisking constantly. This should take about 10 minutes.

As soon as the mixture looks milky, stop whisking, as this prevents the egg filter forming. Let the filter of egg white rise slowly to the top of the pan, then turn down the heat.

With a ladle or spoon handle, make a small hole in the froth so the consomme bubbles through the filter only in that place. Simmer gently for 30 minutes.

Place a scalded tea towel over a clean bowl and carefully ladle the consomme into it, sliding out the filter intact. Do not press on the mixture in the towel. If the consomme is not sparkling clear it can be strained through the cloth and filtered again.

Reheat the consomme in a clean saucepan and serve.

Serves 8

1 Skim solidified fat from chilled soup

2 For every 2 cups of soup use shells and whites of 3 eggs and ¼ cup white wine

3 As soon as the mixture looks milky stop whisking

4 Make a small hole in the froth

5 Place a scalded tea towel over a clean bowl and carefully ladle the consomme into it

Tomato Consomme

Italian Noodle Soup

The flavours of garlic, olive oil and tomato marry together to create a delicious and tempting soup.

2 tablespoons olive oil
⅓ cup chopped bacon
3 cloves garlic, crushed
½ cup chopped tomato
1.25 litres stock or water
250 g linguine pasta, broken
*   into pieces*
freshly ground black pepper
¾ cup Parmesan cheese
1 teaspoon chopped fresh
*   basil or ¼ teaspoon dried*
basil, to garnish

Heat the oil in a pan and cook the bacon and garlic until golden brown. Add the tomato and stock, and bring to the boil. Add the linguine and cook for 15 minutes or until tender. Season to taste, then stir in half the cheese and basil. Sprinkle the remaining cheese over the soup and serve garnished with basil.

Serves 4

Italian Noodle Soup

Minestrone

4 bacon rashers, rind
*   removed*
1½ cups finely chopped
*   parsley*
1 clove garlic, crushed
1 stick celery, chopped
2 potatoes, peeled and
*   chopped*
2 carrots, peeled and
*   chopped*
1 zucchini (courgette),
*   chopped*

125 g green beans, chopped
1 cup dried borlotti beans,
*   soaked overnight*
3 tomatoes, cored, peeled
*   and chopped*
salt and pepper, to taste
1 cup shredded cabbage
1 cup long grain rice, washed
*   well*
grated Parmesan cheese, to
*   garnish*

Chop the bacon very finely and put into a large saucepan with rind, parsley, garlic and celery. Fry gently for 5 minutes, stirring occasionally. Add the potatoes, carrots, zucchini, green beans, borlotti beans and tomatoes to the pan, cover with water and add salt and pepper to taste.

Bring to the boil, cover the pan and simmer for 2 hours or until the dried beans are tender. Check the water level, adding more if necessary.

After the first hour, add the cabbage, then 30 minutes before serving, add the rice and continue simmering. Remove the bacon rind and check the seasoning. Serve with the Parmesan cheese.

Serves 4

Potage Pistou

This recipe works well using quality, canned, peeled tomatoes

200 g green beans, topped
*   and tailed*
600 g tomatoes, peeled
70 g egg noodles
1 clove garlic, crushed
1 teaspoon finely chopped
*   basil*
2 tablespoons olive oil
1 onion, chopped
50 g mild cheese, grated
freshly ground black pepper

Cut the beans into 3 cm lengths and simmer in 1 litre salted water with most of the chopped tomatoes for 15 minutes. Add the egg noodles when the vegetables are almost cooked and cook until tender.

Combine the garlic, basil, olive oil, onion and process or blend with a little liquid until the mixture is smooth and creamy. Add to the tomato and beans and simmer to heat through.

Serve topped with grated cheese, the rest of the chopped tomato and a grinding of black pepper.

Lentil Soup

Tomato Fennel Soup

3 fennel bulbs
90 g butter
1 large onion, chopped
3 garlic cloves, crushed
salt and pepper, to taste
1.6 kg can Italian
* tomatoes*
3 tablespoons Pernod
2 cups canned chicken broth
2 tablespoons chopped
* fennel tops, for garnish*
pitta bread, for serving

Trim fennel and coarsely chop two bulbs. Melt butter in a saucepan, add fennel, onion and garlic and cook until softened. Season to taste. Add tomatoes and juice and cook over low heat for 30 minutes.

Puree the vegetables and return to pan. Finely chop remaining fennel bulb. Cook in 20 g extra butter for 5 minutes. Add to puree with Pernod and chicken broth. Simmer until hot. Serve topped with chopped fennel tops in heated bowls, accompanied by triangles of buttered pitta bread, toasted and sprinkled with herbs.

Serves 6

1 Fennel bulb

2 Using a sharp knife, cut the stems from the bulb. Discard the stems

3 Cut the fennel bulb diagonally into thin slices, discarding the root section if tough

Lentil Soup

375 g red lentils, washed well
¼ cup olive oil
500 g smoked sausage, cut
* into bite-sized pieces*
1 onion, chopped
1 green capsicum (pepper),
* seeded and chopped*
2 cloves garlic, crushed
1 kg tomatoes, cored, peeled
* and chopped*
2 cups beef stock
1 tablespoon Worcestershire
* sauce*
¼ teaspoon oregano
salt and pepper, to taste

Place the lentils in a saucepan and add enough water so that it comes 2.5 cm above the lentils.

Bring to the boil, then reduce the heat and simmer for 20–30 minutes or until the lentils are tender.

Heat half the oil in a saucepan. Add the sausage and cook until browned. Remove from heat and cool slightly. Heat the remaining oil in the cleaned saucepan, add the onion and cook for 4 minutes or until tender. Add the green capsicum and garlic and cook a further 4 minutes. Add the lentils, drained sausage, beef stock and remaining ingredients. Cover and simmer for 45 minutes.

Serves 8

Vegetable Soup

60 g butter
1 tablespoon flour
1 kg tomatoes, cored, peeled
    and chopped
2 carrots, sliced
1 large potato, peeled and
    chopped
1 onion, chopped
½ cup tomato puree
½ cup chicken stock
freshly ground black pepper
grated cheese or croutons, to
    garnish

Melt the butter in a pan, stir in flour and cook for 2 minutes, stirring constantly, until lightly browned. Add the remaining ingredients, bring to the boil, then reduce the heat and simmer for 30 minutes or until the vegetables are tender.

Puree the soup in a food processor or blender. Reheat, then serve garnished with grated cheese or croutons.

Serves 6

Tomato and Smoked Herring Soup

40 g butter
2 smoked herring fillets,
    chopped
750 g tomatoes, cored,
    peeled and chopped
1 clove garlic, crushed
2 tablespoons flour
2 cups hot milk
1¼ cups hot water
salt and pepper, to taste
½ cup cream
1 tablespoon sherry or lemon
    juice

Melt the butter in a saucepan, then remove from the heat. Stir in the fish, tomatoes and garlic. Add the flour and cook, stirring for 1 minute until foaming but not browned. Gradually add the milk and water, stirring constantly until it boils. Season to taste with salt and pepper. Cover the pan and simmer for 20 minutes.

Place in a food processor or blender and process until finely chopped. Add the cream and sherry or lemon juice. Either reheat without boiling and serve hot, or cool and serve chilled.

Serves 4–6

COLD SOUPS

Gazpacho

1 kg tomatoes, cored, peeled
    and finely chopped
2 medium-sized cucumbers,
    peeled, seeded and finely
    chopped
1 onion, finely chopped
1 red capsicum (pepper),
    seeded and finely chopped
2 cloves garlic, crushed
¼ cup olive oil
3 tablespoons white wine
    vinegar
salt and pepper, to taste
pinch cayenne pepper
1½ cups tomato juice
ice cubes
finely chopped parsley, to
    garnish

Combine the tomatoes, cucumbers, onion, capsicum and garlic. Stir in the olive oil, vinegar, salt and pepper, cayenne and tomato juice. Blend well in a food processor or blender, cover and refrigerate until well chilled. Serve with an ice cube in each bowl and garnish with parsley.

Serves 8

Tomato Dill Soup

6 large ripe tomatoes, cored,
    peeled and sliced
1 medium-large onion, sliced
1 clove garlic, crushed
1 pinch salt
freshly ground black pepper,
    to taste
2 tablespoons tomato paste
¼ cup water
3 sprigs fresh dill
½–¾ cup cooked macaroni
1 cup chicken stock
¾ cup fresh cream
small sprigs fresh dill, to
    garnish

Combine tomatoes in a medium-sized saucepan together with the onion, garlic, salt, pepper, tomato paste, water and dill, Cover and cook over a medium heat for about 10 minutes or until the tomatoes have softened.

Process the mixture in a food processor or blender with the cooked pasta, stock and cream until smooth. Pour into a large bowl and refrigerate until chilled. Spoon into soup bowls and serve garnished with dill.

Serves 6

No-cook Tomato Soup

Ice cold soup enriched with vitamins and fibre gives a refreshing lift on hot days. Even more so as no cooking is required!

750 g tomatoes, cored,
*   peeled and chopped*
½ cup finely chopped
*   cucumber*
¼ cup finely chopped onion
¼ cup thinly sliced celery
1 teaspoon sugar
¼ teaspoon garlic salt
¼ teaspoon salt
2 drops Tabasco sauce

Process the tomatoes in a food processor or blender to form a puree. Stir in the remaining ingredients and refrigerate until required. Serve chilled.

Serves 3–4

Orange and Creamy Tomato Soup

850 mL can tomato juice,   *1 cup cream*
*   well chilled*   *freshly ground black pepper*
1 cup freshly squeezed   *1 avocado*
*   orange juice*   *1 tablespoon lemon juice*
1 tablespoon orange rind   *ice cubes*
1 tablespoon finely chopped   *snipped chives, for garnish*
*   chives*

Blend the tomato juice, orange juice, rind and fresh cream. Season to taste. Peel and seed avocado, slice it thinly and sprinkle a little lemon juice over to prevent discolouration. Serve with ice cubes in individual soup bowls. Float the avocado slices on top and garnish with chives.

Serves 4

No-cook Tomato Soup

STARTERS

Crumbed Sardines with Tomato Coulis

It is quite simple to bone a sardine. Grasp the fish by its head and gently pull down and back towards the tail. The bones will come away all attached to the head.

12–18 sardines, cleaned and
   boned
flour seasoned with salt
   and pepper
1 egg
2 tablespoons milk

2 cups fresh breadcrumbs
1 tablespoon grated
   Parmesan cheese
oil for frying
lemon wedges and fresh
   coriander, to garnish

Tomato Coulis

3 tomatoes, cored, peeled,
   seeded and chopped
1 tablespoon chopped
   parsley

1 onion, finely chopped
1 tablespoon tomato paste
salt and pepper, to taste
¼ cup white wine

Coat the sardines in flour, seasoned with salt and pepper. Combine the egg and milk and dip the sardines, then coat them in the breadcrumbs mixed with Parmesan cheese. Set aside for 5 minutes.

To prepare the Tomato Coulis, put all the ingredients into a saucepan, bring to the boil, then simmer for 10 minutes. Set the sauce aside.

Heat the oil in a frying pan until moderately hot and fry the sardines for 1–2 minutes or until golden brown. Drain on absorbent paper. Place 3 sardines onto individual plates and surround with a portion of the Tomato Coulis. Garnish with lemon wedges and fresh coriander.

Serves 4–6

1 Using a small sharp knife, cut the head away from the body

2 Gently pull out the intestine and the backbone

3 Open out the sardine and break the backbone away from the tail end

1 Mix the water, oil and parsley into the combined flour and salt

2 Lightly fold in a stiffly beaten egg white using a large metal spoon

Oyster and Calamari Fritters with Tomato Seafood Sauce

20–30 oysters
16–24 calamari rings
oil, for frying
lemon wedges and parsley,
   to garnish

Batter

½ cup flour
pinch salt
⅓ cup warm water
1 tablespoon oil
1 tablespoon chopped
   parsley
1 egg white, stiffly beaten

Tomato Seafood Sauce

1 cup mayonnaise
dash chilli sauce
2 tablespoons tomato paste
salt and pepper, to taste
½ tablespoon chopped
   chives
1 shallot (spring onion,
   scallion), chopped
1 teaspoon chopped capers

To make the Tomato Seafood Sauce, combine the mayonnaise, chilli sauce, tomato paste, salt and pepper, chives, shallot and capers. Chill until ready for use.

Drain the oysters and calamari on absorbent paper.

To prepare the batter, combine flour and salt in a bowl, then mix in the water, oil and parsley. Fold in the egg white.

Dip each oyster and calamari ring into the batter and deep fry, a few at a time, until crisp and golden. Drain the oysters and calamari on absorbent paper.

Serve the fritters with the Tomato Seafood Sauce and garnish with lemon wedges and parsley.

Serves 4–6

Oyster and Calamari Fritters with
Tomato Seafood Sauce

Mussel Boats

1 kg mussels, scrubbed with
 beards removed
2 tablespoons olive oil
1 onion, finely chopped
1 red capsicum (pepper),
 seeded and chopped
1 green capsicum (pepper),
 seeded and chopped
1 yellow capsicum (pepper),
 seeded and chopped

2 garlic cloves, crushed
50 g smoked ham, finely
 chopped
425 g can tomatoes,
 drained and chopped
pinch saffron threads, soaked
 in ¼ cup dry white wine
salt and pepper, to taste
coriander sprigs, to garnish

Place mussels into a large saucepan and half fill with water.
Bring slowly to the boil and cook for 3–4 minutes. Drain,
reserving 1 cup liquid.

Discard any unopened mussels. Remove the top shell and
loosen the mussel in the bottom shell and reserve. Heat the
oil in a pan and gently fry the onion and capsicums until
softened but not browned. Add the garlic and ham, then stir
in the tomatoes and cook until the mixture thickens. Pour in
the saffron liquid and strained mussel juice. Simmer until
mixture is thick and the liquid has almost evaporated, then
season and cool. Top the mussels with the sauce and serve
the shells on a platter garnished with coriander.

Serves 6

Crayfish with Tomato and Wine

1 x 2 kg live crayfish
salt and cayenne pepper
30 g butter
1 tablespoon oil
1 onion, finely chopped
4 shallots (spring onions,
 scallions), sliced
3 tablespoons brandy

¼ cup white wine
¼ cup fish stock
3 tomatoes, peeled, seeded
 and chopped
1 teaspoon tomato paste or
 granules
extra 30 g butter
fresh herbs, to garnish

Ask the fishmonger to kill the crayfish. Split crayfish in half
lengthwise, cut off the head section and remove and reserve
any roe. Twist off legs and cut tail section into pieces. Season
tail pieces with salt and cayenne pepper.

Heat butter and oil in frying pan. Add crayfish pieces, legs
and onion and cook over a gentle heat for 4 minutes. Add
shallots and cook for a minute more. Pour in the heated
brandy and flame. Shake the pan until the flames die down.
Stir in remaining ingredients except for the butter and herbs.
Bring to the boil, reduce heat and simmer for 15 minutes,
stirring occasionally.

Remove crayfish and keep warm on a serving dish.

Simmer sauce to thicken slightly then stir through the roe
and butter. Push through a sieve or puree in the blender.
Taste and adjust seasonings then reheat. Coat crayfish with
sauce and serve garnished with herbs.

Serves 4

Baked Squid Hoods

Squid that is cleaned and skinned may be purchased from
some fish shops, therefore eliminating the messy task of
removing the ink sac.

8–12 medium-sized to large
 squid hoods
4 anchovies, mashed
1 clove garlic, crushed
1½ cups fresh breadcrumbs

2 tablespoons chopped
 parsley
1 egg, beaten
freshly ground black pepper
3 tablespoons olive oil

Sauce

425 g can tomatoes,
 mashed
1 tablespoon oregano
salt and pepper, to taste
1 red chilli, chopped
2 shallots (spring onions,
 scallions), chopped

Clean the squid, then wash and dry well. Mix the anchovies,
garlic, breadcrumbs, 1 tablespoon of parsley, egg and pepper
together, then fill the squid hoods with the anchovy mixture.
Secure each opening with a toothpick.

Heat the olive oil in a large pan, then add the squid. Cook
until brown, then turn and brown the other side.

Combine all the sauce ingredients and add to the pan.
Bring to the boil, then reduce heat and simmer for 20 minutes. Place 2 squid onto individual serving plates, spoon over
the tomato sauce and serve sprinkled with the rest of the
parsley.

Serves 4–6

Baked Tomato Scallops

1 tablespoon oil
2 cloves garlic, crushed
2 onions, finely chopped
250 g scallops, deveined
2 tablespoons chopped
 parsley
pinch ground cloves
pinch nutmeg
salt and pepper, to taste
2 tablespoons tomato paste
2 tablespoons fresh
 breadcrumbs
1 tablespoon olive oil
4 lemon twists, to garnish

Heat the oil in a frying pan. Add garlic and onions and cook
over low heat for 3 minutes or until tender.

Add the scallops, parsley, cloves, nutmeg, salt, pepper and
tomato paste. Spoon the mixture into 4 shallow ovenproof
dishes. Sprinkle over the breadcrumbs and olive oil. Bake in
an oven preheated to 220°C (425°F) for 15–20 minutes or
until lightly browned. Serve with lemon twists.

Serves 4

1 Line the base of a greased Swiss-roll tin with greased greaseproof paper

2 Using a tea-towel for support, roll up the roulade Swiss-role style, enclosing filling

Tomato and Spinach Roulade

Tomato and Spinach Roulade

6 eggs, separated
6 shallots (spring onions,
    scallions), finely chopped
3 spinach leaves, washed
    and finely chopped
salt and pepper, to taste
¼ cup grated cheese
2 cups tomato pulp

Line a Swiss roll tin with buttered greaseproof paper. Beat the egg yolks until pale and thickened, then add the shallots, spinach, salt and pepper and half the grated cheese.

Whisk the egg whites until stiff peaks form then fold them gently into the egg yolk mixture. Spread the mixture evenly into the tin, smoothing the surface. Bake in an oven preheated to 200°C (400°F) for 30 minutes. Remove the roulade.

Turn roulade onto a damp tea towel and remove the paper from the base. Spread the tomato pulp over, then using the tea towel, pull it slowly upwards so the roulade forms a roll.

Allow the roulade to sit for 1 minute rolled in the tea towel. Remove the tea towel and place the roulade onto a heatproof serving platter. Sprinkle over the remaining cheese and return the roulade to the oven for 2 minutes or until the cheese has melted.

Slice the roulade into portions and arrange on serving plates. Serve with a side salad.

Serves 6

Gnocchi with Tomato Sauce

5 medium-sized potatoes,
    peeled and chopped
1¼ cups flour
2 eggs

Sauce

5 large ripe tomatoes, cored,
    peeled and chopped
1 tablespoon tomato paste
salt and pepper, to taste
60 g butter
grated Parmesan cheese
chopped parsley, to garnish

Boil the potatoes until tender, then drain and mash. Fold in the flour and eggs, then set the mixture aside to cool slightly.

To make the sauce, put the tomatoes, tomato paste, salt, pepper and butter into a shallow pan and bring to the boil, then reduce the heat and simmer for 20 minutes. Set aside until required.

Form the potato dough into small walnut-sized balls, pressing one side of the ball against a grater to form a pattern.

Bring a large pan of salted water to the boil, drop 4–6 gnocchi into the water and cook at a simmer for 10–12 minutes or until the gnocchi float to the surface. Remove with a slotted spoon and drain. Continue in this way until all the gnocchi are cooked.

Divide the gnocchi between 4–6 individual serving or gratin dishes. Spoon over the reserved Tomato Sauce, then sprinkle with the Parmesan cheese. Bake in an oven preheated to 200°C (400°F) for 10–15 minutes or until bubbling and brown. Sprinkle with parsley and serve.

Serves 4–6

1 Mould the potato mixture into walnut-sized balls, using lightly floured fingers

2 Poach Potato Gnocchi in boiling salted water. Remove with a slotted spoon and drain on absorbent paper

3 Place Potato Gnocchi in a greased ovenproof dish and cover with hot tomato sauce

4 Sprinkle over grated cheese before grilling

Stroganoff Choux

Choux Puffs
1 cup water
75 g butter
1 cup flour
pinch salt
4 x 60 g eggs, beaten

Filling
125 g butter
1 onion, finely chopped
500 g fillet steak, sliced thinly
250 g mushrooms, sliced
freshly ground black pepper
2/3 cup water
2 beef stock cubes
2 tablespoons tomato paste
2 teaspoons cornflour
300 mL sour (dairy soured)
    cream
watercress and tomato
    wedges, to garnish

Put the water and butter into a saucepan and bring to the boil. As soon as it boils, add the flour and salt, stirring constantly until the mixture forms a ball. Remove from the heat and set aside for 10 minutes or until cooled slightly.

Gradually add the beaten eggs to the dough, beating well after each addition, so the mixture is smooth, firm and glossy.

Drop heaped tablespoonsful onto a lightly greased baking tray and bake in an oven preheated to 200°C (400°F) for 10 minutes. Reduce the heat to 180°C (350°F) and cook for a further 20 minutes or until the puffs are golden brown. When just cooked, insert the point of a sharp knife into the side of each puff then leave in the oven for a further 5 minutes. Remove to a cake rack to cool slightly.

To make the filling, heat the butter in a pan and fry the onion gently for 2 minutes, then add the steak and cook to seal. Add the mushrooms and season with pepper. Cook, stirring occasionally, for 15 minutes. Combine the water, stock cubes, tomato paste and cornflour. Stir into the steak and cook until thickened. Gradually add the cream, stirring to mix evenly.

To serve, cut the choux puffs in half placing the base on the plate. Fill the centre with the stroganoff mix, then top with the choux lid. Garnish with the watercress and tomato wedges.

Serves 6

Deep-fried Vegetables with Tomato Dip

A healthy entree suggestion. The vegetable shapes by themselves are attractive, and further enhanced by the tangy tomato dip.

Batter
1 cup chick pea flour
salt and pepper, to taste
½ teaspoon chilli powder
½ teaspoon bicarbonate of
    soda
water
3 cups oil, for frying

Vegetables
1 small potato, peeled and
    sliced
1 eggplant (aubergine), cut
    into thin slices
1 onion, sliced
1 green capsicum (pepper),
    seeded and sliced into
    rings
3–4 cauliflower florets,
    separated into smaller
    florets

Tomato dip
1 cup fresh tomato puree
1¼ cups natural yoghurt
salt and pepper, to taste
¼ teaspoon cumin
1 tablespoon chopped fresh
    coriander, to garnish

Combine the flour, salt and pepper, chilli powder and bicarbonate of soda, then gradually whisk in enough water to form a smooth batter. Heat the oil in a deep fryer or large saucepan.

To make the dip, combine the pureed tomato, yoghurt, salt and pepper, and cumin. Just before serving, garnish with the coriander.

Dip the vegetables into the batter, then fry in small batches until golden brown. Drain on absorbent paper. Serve the fried vegetables on a plate with the Tomato Dip.

Serves 6

Tomato and Ham Pate

4 stuffed olives
2 cups cream
¾ cup finely minced ham
1 tablespoon tomato paste
t tablespoon sherry
freshly ground black pepper
dash curry powder
1 cup beef stock
1 cup tomato juice
½ teaspoon paprika
3 teaspoons gelatine
2 slices bread, crusts
*   removed*

Slice the olives into quarters and arrange the slices on the base of four wet 1-cup moulds.

Whip the cream until soft peaks form, fold in the ham, tomato paste, sherry, pepper and curry powder.

Put the stock, tomato juice, paprika and gelatine into a saucepan over low heat and cook until the gelatine has dissolved. Cool. When the mixture starts to set fold in the flavoured cream. Spoon the mixture into the moulds and chill in the refrigerator for 1–2 hours, then unmould onto individual plates. Toast the bread, then cut into 4 triangles. Place 2 trianges on each plate and serve.

Serves 4

Savoury Tomato Cases

3 slices of bacon, chopped,
*   with rind removed*
1 small onion, chopped
1 large tomato, cored,
*   peeled, seeded and*
*   chopped*
1 cup corn kernels
salt and pepper, to taste
pinch of sugar
1 tablespoon finely chopped
*   fresh basil leaves*
10 savoury pastry cases or
*   breadcases, for serving*
cherry tomatoes, thinly
*   sliced, and black olives,*
*   finely sliced, for garnish*

Cook the bacon until crisp, then transfer it to absorbent paper to drain. Cook the onion in the bacon fat for 3 minutes or until soft. Add the tomato and corn and cook together until tender. Season with salt and pepper and a pinch of sugar, then stir in the bacon and basil.

Fill the prepared cases with the filling and bake in an oven preheated to 180°C (350°F) for 10 minutes or until heated through. Garnish with the cherry tomatoes and slivers of black olives.

Makes 8

Tomato Souffle

When whisking egg whites, use a clean, dry bowl to achieve a light egg-white foam very quickly.

45 g butter
¼ cup flour
1 cup milk
salt and pepper, to taste
pinch cayenne pepper
45 g cheddar cheese, grated
45 g Parmesan cheese,
*   grated*
4 egg yolks
5 egg whites

Filling

30 g butter
3 shallots (spring onions,
*   scallions), chopped*
1 cup fresh tomato puree

Melt the butter in a heavy-based pan, then whisk in the flour. Cook for 1–2 minutes until foaming but not brown, then gradually whisk in the milk. Season with salt and pepper. Bring the sauce to the boil, stirring constantly until the mixture thickens. Remove from the heat and allow to cool slightly.

Add the cheeses gradually, mixing well. Set aside. Lightly grease 6 x 2 cup souffle dishes. Tie a collar of greased paper around each dish so that the collar stands 7.5 cm higher than the dish.

To make the filling, melt the butter in a medium-sized saucepan. Add tomato pulp and shallots and cook over medium heat for 2 minutes.

Beat the egg yolks into cheese mixture. Whisk egg whites in a clean dry bowl until soft peaks form, then fold through egg yolk and cheese mixture. Pour ½ cup of cheese mixture into base of each souffle dish, then spoon equal portions of tomato mixture on top. Cover with the remaining souffle mixture. Bake in an oven preheated to 190°C (375°F) for 10–12 minutes or until well risen and golden brown. When cooked remove the collar and serve immediately.

Serves 6

Tomato Mousse

1 cup clear aspic, flavoured
with sherry
250 g tomatoes, cored,
peeled, seeded and diced
3 tablespoons tomato sauce
2 tablespoons tomato juice
3 tablespoons tomato paste
cayenne pepper
pinch sugar
1 teaspoon gelatine
3 tablespoons hot beef stock
1 cup cream, whipped
fresh dill, to garnish

Pour a little of the clear aspic into 6 x 1 cup moulds and tilt from side to side to coat evenly. Place in refrigerator while preparing mousse. Rub 125 g tomatoes through a sieve, add sauce, juice and paste. Season. Dissolve gelatine in stock and whisk into mixture. Set to a soft gel and whisk in one quarter of the whipped cream and then fold in remainder. Fold in remaining diced tomato. Pour into moulds. Set in refrigerator until firm.

Unmould and serve with prawns and cherry tomatoes. Garnished with fresh dill.

Serves 6

Kidneys in Sherry Tomato Sauce

1 kg sheeps' kidneys
salt, to taste
2 tablespoons olive oil

Sauce

3 tablespoons olive oil
1 onion, finely chopped
1 clove garlic, crushed
1 bay leaf
1 tablespoon flour
½ cup beef stock
2 tablespoons tomato puree
pinch nutmeg
1 tablespoon finely chopped
parsley
salt and pepper, to taste
⅔ cup dry sherry
2 slices bread, crusts
removed
1 tablespoon oil

Place the kidneys into a bowl, cover with water and soak for 2 hours, changing the water twice. Drain, them remove the skin, core and white tissue from the kidneys. Cut kidneys into thin slices, and season lightly with salt.

Heat the olive oil in a pan and gently brown the kidneys for 5 minutes over medium heat. Combine all the ingredients for the sauce and add to the pan. Simmer for 5 minutes.

Cut each slice of bread into 4 triangles, then fry in hot oil until crisp. Drain on absorbent paper. Serve the kidneys on individual plates with 2 bread triangles on the side.

Serves 4

Baked Eggs Melange

12 hard-boiled eggs, shelled
810 g can tomato pieces
120 g butter
1 onion, chopped
1 capsicum (pepper), seeded
and chopped
1 cup chopped celery
2 tablespoons flour
salt and pepper, to taste
cayenne pepper, to taste
1 cup White Sauce (see
recipe)
365 g can champignons,
chopped
½ cup fresh breadcrumbs
½ cup grated cheese
parsley, finely chopped

Chop the eggs roughly. Strain tomatoes, reserving the juice. Melt half the butter in a pan and gently fry the onion, capsicum and celery until tender. Add the flour and tomatoes, stirring until the mixture thickens. Add the reserved tomato juice and seasonings, then bring the liquid to the boil. Stir in the White Sauce, chopped eggs and champignons.

Spoon the mixture into individual serving dishes or an oblong casserole dish, then top with breadcrumbs and dot with the remaining butter. Bake in an oven preheated to 220°C (425°F) for 10 minutes or until brown and bubbling. Sprinkle over the grated cheese and parsley.

Serves 8

1 Add tomatoes and flour to fried onion, capsicum and celery

2 Pour in the tomato juice and seasonings

3 Stir in the white sauce

4 Stir in the chopped eggs and champignons

Tomato Mousse

Savoury Pancake Parcel

Pancake Batter
1 cup wholemeal flour
1¼ cups milk
1 egg
oil for frying

Filling
3–4 tablespoons oil
2 onions, finely chopped
180 g mushrooms, sliced
3 tomatoes, cored, peeled and
*   chopped*
750 g pork and veal mince
1 clove garlic, crushed
1 tablespoon tomato puree
¼ cup chopped fresh basil or
1 tablespoon dried basil
1 teaspoon dried oregano
1 teaspoon grated nutmeg
1 tablespoon Parmesan
*   cheese*

To make the pancake batter, place the flour, milk and egg into a processor or blender and blend until smooth. Alternatively, sift the flour and salt together into a large bowl. Make a well in the centre and drop in the egg. Add 200 mL of milk and gradually stir the flour into the liquid, adding more milk if necessary. Beat until smooth.

Heat a little oil in a crepe pan, turning the pan so it is evenly coated with oil. Pour in 2–3 tablespoons of batter, tilting the pan to spread the batter thinly. Cook the bottom side for 2–3 minutes or until golden, then cook the other side. Repeat until all the pancakes have been cooked, keeping them warm in very low oven until required.

Meanwhile, prepare the filling. Heat the oil in a large pan,

1 Overlap the pancakes to line the base and sides of a greased ovenproof dish

2 Spoon the filling into the centre

3 Cover with the remaining pancakes. Turn over the edges of the pancakes to enclose the filling

then saute the onions for 5 minutes or until soft but not browned. Remove with a slotted spoon and reserve. Gently fry the mushrooms in the same oil until soft and reserve. Fry the tomatoes until soft and reserve also. Add the mince to the oil and cook, stirring until the mince has turned light brown and broken up. Stir in the garlic, tomato puree, herbs and nutmeg, and cook until the meat has browned. Spoon out excess fat. Return the reserved ingredients to the pan and reheat.

Grease a shallow, ovenproof dish. Line base and sides with pancakes, making sure they come above the edges of the dish. Spoon the mixture into the centre spreading it out evenly, then cover with the remaining pancakes. Turn over the edges of the pancakes to enclose the filling and sprinkle over the cheese. Cover with aluminium foil and heat in a low oven, 150°C (300°F) for 15 minutes or until ready to serve. Serve with salad.

Serves 6

Veal and Salami Crepes

Crepe Mixture
1¼ cups flour
pinch of salt
3 eggs
1½ cups milk
1 tablespoon brandy
10 g butter, melted
extra butter

Filling
⅓ cup olive oil
500 g veal mince
125 g salami, finely chopped
3 shallots (spring onions,
*   scallions), chopped*
¼ cup tomato paste
½ cup dry white wine
salt and pepper to taste

Topping
⅔ cup grated Parmesan
*   cheese*
pinch nutmeg
1 tablespoon breadcrumbs
40 g butter, melted
cherry tomatoes and
*   watercress, to garnish*

To make the crepes, combine the flour and salt in a bowl, then gradually add the eggs, milk, brandy and melted butter, whisking to form a smooth batter.

Place 1 tablespoon of butter into a crepe pan or frying pan, tilting the pan over the heat until it is evenly coated with butter. Pour 1 tablespoon of the batter into the hot pan. Cook until brown on one side, then turn and cook until golden. Cook all the crepes and stack with layers of greaseproof paper in between. Keep warm in the oven while preparing filling.

To prepare the filling; heat the oil in a large pan, then add the veal, salami and shallots. Cook over high heat stirring occasionally, until well browned. Add the tomato paste, wine and season with salt and pepper. Cook over a medium heat, stirring from time to time until the excess moisture evaporates.

Place 2 tablespoons of the meat mixture onto each crepe, then roll up and place, fold-side down, into baking dish. Sprinkle over the Parmesan cheese, nutmeg and breadcrumbs, then pour over the melted butter. Bake in an oven preheated to 200°C (400°F) for 10–15 minutes or until the mixture bubbles and browns. Serve 2 crepes to each person, garnished with cherry tomatoes and watercress.

Serves 4–6

Open Sandwiches

Open sandwiches are the ideal snack solution: they are both healthy and quick to prepare. Why cover colourful, fresh ingredients with a second slice of bread when they can be served in delicious Danish style?

Bread Suggestions
The following breads make delicious bases for open sandwiches, with flavour and texture contributing to the sandwich appeal. These breads will stay fresher for longer.
• Pumpernickel
• Rye or sour bread
• Sliced Loaf Brioche

Suggested Toppings
• Basil Butter (see recipe), sliced tomato, finely chopped shallots and strips of prosciutto
• lettuce, halved cherry tomatoes, tuna, finely sliced onion and mayonnaise
• sliced ham, sliced tomato, Swiss cheese, chives, pecans
• ricotta cheese, tomato wedges topped with strips of smoked turkey breast and mustard cress.

Tomatoes are a colourful and flavoursome addition with Open Sandwiches

Tomato and Eggplant Farcis

810 g can peeled
  tomatoes
6 medium-sized eggplants
  (aubergine)
3 onions, sliced
200 g mushrooms, diced
2 cloves garlic, crushed
200 g mozzarella cheese,
  sliced
⅓ cup olive oil
1 tablespoon finely chopped
  parsley, for garnish

Drain the tomatoes retaining the juice. Cut the eggplants in half, lengthways, and scoop out the flesh leaving a 1 cm thick shell. Roughly chop the scooped out flesh and combine with onions, mushrooms and garlic.

Heat the oil and fry the eggplant mixture, cooking until softened. Add enough tomato juice to moisten, then simmer until the mixture has thickened.

Spoon mixture into the eggplant shells. Place 2 tomatoes in each shell, cover with slices of mozzarella and bake at 180°C (350°F) for 25 minutes. Serve garnished with parsley.

Serves 12

SALADS AND DRESSINGS

A salad without tomato is rather like a garden without flowers. Tomatoes provide salads with colour, aroma, texture and taste. And of course they are filled with natural goodness too. This salad section takes the tomato and uses it in a variety of simply delicious salady ways from crudites served for a change with a tomato dip or a pasta salad served with a pesto dressing to traditional summer salads such as Tomato and Onion, Salad Nicoise and that perennial favourite — a Lettuce Bowl Salad that's ideal for buffets and barbecue entertaining. But, the vital ingredient in salad making is invention. Take our ideas and let your own grow out of them.

Tomato Citrus Salad (front), Tomato and Onion Salad

Tomato Citrus Salad

Serve this tangy salad as an accompaniment to cold ham or poultry.

*1 kg tomatoes, cored, peeled
    and thickly sliced
1 teaspoon caster sugar
salt and pepper, to taste
4 oranges
⅓ cup French Dressing (see
    recipe)
1 tablespoon snipped chives,
    to garnish*

Sprinkle the tomatoes with the sugar and season with salt and pepper. Carefully remove the rind from one orange and cut into julienne strips. Blanch the strips in boiling water for 3–4 minutes, then drain and refresh with cold water. Set aside. Peel the oranges, removing all the pith, then cut them into segments.

Arrange the tomato slices and orange segments on a serving dish and sprinkle over the French Dressing. Garnish with the strips of rind and snipped chives and serve well-chilled.

Serves 6–8

Salade Nicoise

A typically French salad made with a combination of garden fresh ingredients and tuna.

*1 cos lettuce
1 mignonette lettuce (soft
    head)
1 small onion, thinly sliced
2 tablespoons capers*

*420 g canned tuna in brine,
    drained
4 ripe tomatoes, cut into
    wedges
4 anchovy fillets, cut into fine
    strips*

Dressing

*1 tablespoon tarragon
    vinegar
1 tablespoon olive oil
1 clove garlic, peeled and
    lightly pressed
salt and freshly ground
    pepper
1 tablespoon finely chopped
    parsley*

Wash the lettuce well in cold water and separate into leaves. Cover and refrigerate for 20 minutes.

Tear each lettuce leaf in half and arrange in a salad bowl with the remaining salad ingredients on top.

Combine the dressing ingredients in a screw-topped jar and shake until blended. Remove the garlic clove before serving. Just before serving, sprinkle the dressing over the salad and toss gently to combine.

Serves 6

Greek Salad

*1 lettuce
4 ripe tomatoes, cut into
    wedges
4 shallots (spring onions,
    scallions), finely chopped
1 onion, thinly sliced
1 green capsicum (pepper),
    seeded and sliced
12 large black olives
100 g feta cheese, cut into
    cubes*

Dressing

*3 tablespoons olive oil
1 tablespoon lemon juice
pinch oregano
salt and freshly ground black
    pepper, to taste*

Wash the lettuce and tear into bite-sized pieces. Mix with the remaining ingredients in a salad bowl and toss through gently.

Combine all the dressing ingredients in a screw-topped jar and shake until well blended. Just before serving sprinkle over the salad.

Serves 6

Tomato and Onion Salad

A colourful and refreshing salad that's popular for summer barbecues.

*6 tomatoes, cored and peeled
1 large purple onion, thinly
    sliced
⅓ cup Vinaigrette (see
    recipe).
2 tablespoons chopped
    parsley
1 tablespoon snipped chives,
    to garnish*

Thinly slice the tomatoes and arrange on a flat plate. Push the onion into rings and arrange over the tomatoes.

Whisk the dressing and parsley together and pour it over the tomatoes. Cover and chill until serving time. Serve, sprinkled with the chives.

Serves 4–6

Salad Nicoise (front), Farmhouse Salad

Farmhouse Salads

½ bunch curly endive
1 bunch radicchio
1 iceberg lettuce (crisphead),
*   outer leaves removed*
1 clove garlic, peeled and
*   lightly pressed*
4 bacon rashers, rind
*   removed and chopped*
¼ cup pine nuts

2 cups deep-fried croutons
1 tablespoon finely chopped
*   basil*
4 tomatoes, cut into wedges
juice of ½–1 lemon, to taste
1 teaspoon vinegar
1–2 tablespoons virgin olive
*   oil*

Rinse the endive, radicchio and lettuce in cold water, drain well and chill, covered, until ready to use.

Rub the pressed garlic clove around the inside of a salad bowl then line it with lettuce leaves. Tear the remaining lettuce, endive and radicchio into bite-sized pieces and add to the bowl. Sprinkle over the bacon, pine nuts, croutons and basil. Add the tomatoes and toss through until combined.

Sprinkle the salad with lemon juice and vinegar, cover and refrigerate. Just before serving sprinkle the olive oil.

Serves 6

Crudites with Tomato Dip

Tomato Dip
¼ cup mayonnaise
300 mL sour (dairy soured)
*   cream*
2 tablespoons natural
*   yoghurt*
3 tablespoons tomato paste
3 tablespoons tomato
*   chutney*
1 clove garlic, crushed
¼ teaspoon cayenne pepper
freshly ground black pepper,
*   to taste*

Crudites
2 carrots, peeled
3 sticks celery
4 zucchini (courgettes)
300 g broccoli, broken into
*   florets*
125 g button mushrooms
250 g cherry tomatoes

Combine the Tomato Dip ingredients, mixing until well-blended and smooth. Spoon into a serving dish, cover and chill until serving time.

To make the crudite, cut the carrots, celery and zucchini into match-stick lengths. Rinse the remaining ingredients with cold water. Place the dip in the centre of a platter, surrounded with the vegetables.

Serves 6

Cherry Tomatoes with Basil

Sweet basil and tomatoes are garden friends, the herb protecting the fruit from disease and insects. The flavour of tomatoes sprinkled with basil makes a piquant salad.

2 punnets cherry tomatoes,
*   washed and chilled*
⅓ cup Vinaigrette (see recipe)
1 clove garlic, peeled and
*   lightly pressed*
1 tablespoon fresh basil
*   leaves, shredded, to*
*   garnish*

Place the tomatoes in a deep salad bowl. Steep the garlic in the vinaigrette for 30 minutes, then remove and discard. Pour the dressing over the tomatoes and stir lightly until coated. Sprinkle with fresh basil.

Serves 6

Poinsettia Salad

The vivid red poinsettia leaves look right royal in the garden. In the following salad, tomatoes and leafy green vegetables are arranged to resemble this flower. Serve in individual glass bowls.

1 cos lettuce
small bunch curly endive
4 slices prosciutto (Parma
*   ham)*
6 ripe tomatoes, cut into fine
*   wedges*

Dressing
2 tablespoons finely chopped
*   chives*
1 tablespoon lemon juice
1 tablespoon olive oil
freshly ground pepper
2 tablespoons tarragon
*   vinegar*

Wash the lettuce and separate into leaves. Arrange leaves radiating out from the centre of the salad bowls. Place the endive leaves over the cos lettuce.

Starting at the centre of the circle arrange the tomato wedges so that they form lines radiating out from the centre. Roll the slices of prosciutto and place in the centre. Combine the dressing ingredients and sprinkle over salad before serving.

Serves 4

Tabouli

Packet tabouli mix is now available from many supermarkets. Enhance its flavour by adding extra lemon juice, garlic and herbs. This recipe is for those who love to make their own tabouli with sun-ripened tomatoes and fresh herbs.

1 cup burghul (cracked
   wheat), well washed and
   drained
1 lettuce
2 cups finely chopped parsley
4 shallots (spring onions,
   scallions), finely chopped
½ cup finely chopped mint

¼ cup lemon juice
salt and pepper, to taste
3 ripe tomatoes, cored,
   peeled and finely chopped
¼ cup olive oil
lemon wedges, for garnish

Place burghul in a bowl with enough water to cover and soak for 30 minutes. Drain well, pressing out the excess water.

Wash the lettuce, cut away the core and separate into leaves. Line a salad bowl with some of the lettuce and shred the rest, using a sharp knife. Combine with the remaining ingredients and spoon into the salad bowl. Garnish with lemon before serving.

Serves 6–8

Cold Pasta with Gazpacho

500 g pasta bows
2 green capsicum (peppers),
   seeded and chopped
1 Spanish onion, chopped
6 shallots (spring onions,
   scallions), thinly sliced

1 cup black olives, stoned
   and sliced
1 cup finely chopped Italian
   parsley
1 cup chopped fresh mint

Gazpacho Dressing

½ cup olive oil
½ cup red wine vinegar
½ teaspoon ground cumin
2 cloves garlic, crushed
5 medium tomatoes, peeled,
   seeded and chopped

1 large cucumber, peeled,
   seeded and chopped
salt and freshly ground black
   pepper, to taste
1 teaspoon chilli sauce

Cook the pasta bows in 3 litres of boiling water until tender, about 10–12 minutes. Drain well and place in a large bowl.

Make the salad dressing by combining the olive oil, vinegar, cummin, garlic, half the tomatoes and cucumber, salt, pepper and chilli sauce in a food processor or blender. Process until smooth.

Toss the dressing through the hot pasta. Allow to cool to room temperature, stirring occasionally to coat the pasta evenly with the dressing.

Spoon the pasta onto a large platter and arrange the remaining ingredients in concentric circles over the top.

Serves 10–12

Pasta Salad with Pesto Dressing

Pesto is an Italian sauce flavoured with basil and Parmesan cheese. Once made, the dressing can be kept refrigerated for up to 3 months. Use to add extra flavour to vegetables, poached fish or baby potatoes.

350 g green tagliatelle
   noodles
1 cup mustard cress
200 g cherry tomatoes
4 slices leg ham, diced

Pesto Dressing

1 clove garlic, crushed
¼ cup finely chopped fresh
   basil
¼ cup finely chopped parsley
1 tablespoon grated
   Parmesan cheese

¼ cup ground pine nuts or
   walnuts
¼ cup olive oil
3 tablespoons white wine or
   tarragon vinegar

Cook pasta in 4 litres of boiling salted water for 10–12 minutes until the pasta is 'al dente'. Adding 1 tablespoon of oil to the water will prevent the pasta from sticking or boiling over. Drain well and rinse in cold water and drain again.

Place pasta into a salad bowl with the remaining salad ingredients. Combine all the Pesto Dressing ingredients in a large screw-topped jar and shake well to combine. Sprinkle over the salad and toss before serving.

Serves 4

Hot Vegetable Salad with Basil

1 green capsicum (pepper),
   seeded and sliced
300 g cauliflower, cut into
   florets
200 g beans, strung
300 g cherry tomatoes
60 g butter, melted
salt and freshly ground black
   pepper
10 fresh basil leaves cut into
   fine ribbons
1 teaspoon French mustard
sprigs of fresh basil, for
   garnish

Blanch the capsicum, cauliflower and beans in boiling water for 3 minutes. Drain well then place in a heatproof dish.

Scatter over the tomatoes.

Combine the butter, salt, pepper, basil and mustard. Drizzle this dressing over the vegetables and bake at 180°C (350°F) for 10 minutes. Serve at once garnished with the extra basil.

Serves 6

Lettuce Bowl Salad

As an elegant addition to your next buffet, serve these intriguing salads which are contained within their own lettuce cup 'bowls'.

1 iceberg lettuce (crisphead)
6 bacon rashers
3 tomatoes, sliced
1 endive, divided into leaves
6 quail eggs, hard-boiled and
    shelled
12 chives, snipped in half
1 tablespoon pine nuts

Dressing

½ cup mayonnaise
1 teaspoon French mustard
1 teaspoon grated lemon rind
freshly ground black pepper

Wash the lettuce and separate into leaves. Using a small knife, cut away the stem end of the leaf. Arrange the lettuce cups on a salad platter.

Thread the bacon onto skewers and grill until crisp and cooked. Arrange a few tomato slices in each lettuce cup. Lean an endive leaf against the inside edge of each lettuce cup. Remove the bacon from the skewers and arrange in the salad cups with the remaining salad ingredients. Combine all the dressing ingredients, mixing until well blended. Spoon a little over the salad just before serving.

Serves 6

Tomatoes with Yoghurt

This light and summery salad is low on kilojoules and makes a refreshing accompaniment to barbequed or roast meat.

⅓ cup natural yoghurt
1 tablespoon mayonnaise
2 teaspoons chopped dill
1 tablespoon chopped shallot
    (spring onion, scallion)
2 teaspoons lemon juice
freshly ground black pepper
3 large ripe tomatoes, peeled
    and sliced
3 sprigs fresh dill, for garnish

Blend together yoghurt, mayonnaise, dill, shallot, lemon juice and pepper. Cover and refrigerate for 30 minutes. Arrange the tomato slices in an overlapping pattern on a serving platter. Refrigerate and just before serving spoon over the yoghurt dressing and garnish with dill.

Serves 6

Lettuce Bowl Salad

Tomato Granita

8 tomatoes, peeled, seeded
    and finely chopped
2 shallots (spring onions,
    scallions), chopped
1 stick celery, chopped
1 clove garlic, crushed
1 cucumber, peeled and
    finely diced
1 teaspoon finely chopped
    mint

Strain the tomatoes to remove excess liquid. Combine with shallots, celery and garlic. Pour the mixture into metal freezer trays and freeze for 8 hours. Remove from the freezer about 10 minutes before serving to soften the ice a little.

Break the ice up with a fork and stir in the cucumber and mint. Spoon into individual glass dishes and serve.

Serves 2

Vinaigrette

This recipe is the basis of many fine salad dressings that add pizzazz to leafy green vegetables. To vary the flavour or add a gourmet touch, use the unique flavours of walnut, almond, or rape oil blended with a little herb or strawberry vinegar. These are all quite strong, so use sparingly and combine with vegetable oil or white vinegar to make the correct proportions.

½ cup white wine vinegar
salt and freshly ground black
    pepper
1 cup olive oil (or a
    combination of half olive
    oil and half vegetable oil)

Combine all the ingredients in a screw-topped jar or blender and shake or process until well combined.

Makes 1½ cups

French Dressing

French Dressing is a must with green salad vegetables, tomatoes and cucumber.

¼ cup white wine vinegar
salt
freshly ground black pepper
½ teaspoon sugar
½ teaspoon mustard powder
1 clove garlic, peeled and
    lightly pressed
½ cup olive oil

Combine vinegar, salt and pepper, sugar, mustard and garlic in a screw-topped jar or blender. Shake or process until well-blended. Gradually add the oil and mix until combined.

Makes ¾ cup

LIGHT MEALS AND SIDE DISHES

Tomatoes are ideal for delicious light meals and tasty side dishes.
Slice them and add a basil vinaigrette; top them with Mozzarella
and grill to heat through and you have an appetising and
effortless meal the whole family can enjoy.
Some of the recipes in this section can be prepared in a matter
of minutes — others take a little more time; but all are ideal for
those occasions when no one is very hungry or when
there's not a lot of time.
The side dish is there to complement the main meal — in colour,
texture and flavour. The red of the tomato does the job perfectly.
Hot or cold, tomato side dishes are delicious with meat, chicken,
fish and vegetarian meals on just about every occasion.
These recipes can be prepared with very little effort to create the
perfect accompaniment to family meals and when entertaining.

Pissaladiere

Pissaladiere

Pastry
2 cups self raising flour
pinch salt
60 g butter, diced
60 g lard, diced
3–6 tablespoons iced water

Topping
3 tablespoons oil
2 large onions, thinly sliced
1 clove garlic, crushed
500 g tomatoes, cored,
    peeled and sliced
freshly ground black pepper,
    to taste
60 g canned anchovies,
    drained
12 black olives, halved and
    pitted
extra oil, for brushing

To make the pastry, sift the flour and salt in a bowl. Add the butter and lard and rub in quickly with the fingertips until the mixture resembles fine breadcrumbs. Add just enough water to make the dough smooth and pliable. Turn on to a floured surface and knead gently for a few minutes or until smooth.

Roll out to fit a greased 19 x 28 cm Swiss roll tin. Line the tin with pastry and refrigerate until required.

To make the topping, heat the oil in a large saucepan and gently fry the onions and garlic for 10 minutes. Spread the mixture over the dough, then top with the tomatoes. Season lightly with pepper.

Arrange the anchovies over the tomatoes in a lattice pattern, and fill the diamonds created with the olives. Brush lightly with oil and bake in an oven preheated to 200°C (400°F) for 25–30 minutes.

Variations: Cover tomatoes with salami slices and decorate with strips of cheese.

Serves 4–6

Wholemeal Pizza Dough

4 cups wholemeal self-raising
    flour
salt and pepper, to taste
30 g butter
1½ cups cold water

Season the flour, then rub in the butter until the mixture resembles coarse breadcrumbs. Make a well in the centre, pour in the water and mix with a butter knife to form a firm dough. Knead lightly for 2–3 minutes, then divide the dough in half.

Roll out each portion to fit a lightly oiled 30 cm pizza tray, and top with one of the following pizza recipes.

Serves 4–6

Vegetarian Pizza Topping

oil, for deep frying
1 small eggplant (aubergine),
    cut into 1 cm dice
½ small cauliflower, cut into
    small florets
1 quantity Wholemeal Pizza
    Dough (see recipe)
Fresh Tomato Sauce (see
    recipe)
1½ cups grated Mozzarella
    cheese
450 g canned unsweetened
    pineapple pieces
3 small zucchini (courgettes),
    cut into thin rings
½ red capsicum (pepper), cut
    into strips
½ green capsicum (pepper),
    cut into strips
12 black olives, pitted
salt and pepper, to taste

Heat the oil in a deep pan and deep fry the eggplant and cauliflower until golden. Drain well on absorbent paper.

Spread the prepared pizza dough with the tomato sauce and cover it with the grated cheese. Top with the eggplant, cauliflower, pineapple pieces, zucchini, capsicum, olives and any remaining cheese. Season to taste.

Bake in an oven preheated to 190°C (375°F) for 25–30 minutes or until the dough is well risen and golden.

Serves 4–6

Pizza Marinara

1 quantity of Wholemeal
    Pizza Dough (see recipe)
Fresh Tomato Sauce (see
    recipe)
1½ cups grated Mozzarella
    cheese
250 g uncooked prawns,
    peeled
250 g thick fish fillets, sliced
3 seafood sticks
12 mussels, shelled
12 smoked or fresh oysters
salt and pepper, to taste
2 shallots (spring onions,
    scallions), finely chopped
1 tablespoon finely chopped
    parsley
lemon twists, to garnish

Spread the prepared pizza dough with the tomato sauce, then cover with the grated cheese. Arrange the seafood over the cheese and season with salt and pepper. Sprinkle over the shallots and parsley. Bake in an oven preheated to 190°C (375°F) for 10 minutes, then reduce the heat to 175°C (345°F) for 10–15 minutes more. Garnish with lemon twists.

Serves 4–6

Vegetarian Pizza Topping (front), Pizza Marinara

Machacado

Use left-over roast beef for this spicy Mexican recipe.

Tortillas
3 cups flour
¾ teaspoon baking powder
¾ teaspoon salt
75 g lard, diced
1 cup hot water

Meat Sauce
2 tablespoons oil
2 cups finely minced roast
  beef
½ onion, chopped
2 tomatoes, cored, peeled
  and chopped
salt, to taste
2 small red chillies, seeded
  and finely chopped
6 eggs, beaten

To make the tortillas, sift the flour, baking powder and salt into a large bowl. Cut in the lard using two butter knives until the mixture is the texture of fine breadcrumbs. Slowly pour the hot water over the surface, then quickly mix it in with a fork, just until the dough holds together. Leave in the refrigerator in a greased bowl covered with plastic wrap for 1 hour.

Meanwhile to make the sauce, heat the oil in a saucepan, add the meat stirring constantly. Cook over high heat 5 minutes or until browned, then reduce the heat and add the onion. Cook for 5 minutes, stirring constantly or until the onion is soft and golden. Stir in the tomatoes, salt and chillies. Cook uncovered, stirring occasionally for 20–25 minutes or until mixture has thickened. Mix in the eggs and heat, stirring constantly, until the eggs have cooked.

Turn the dough onto a floured board and knead for 5 minutes or until the dough is smooth and elastic. Pinch off small pieces, form them into small balls the size of a walnut then roll out into thin circles. Quickly fry the circles in a lightly greased pan until brown on both sides.

Keep the cooked tortillas warm by covering with aluminium foil while preparing the remaining batches. Spoon the chilli meat sauce over the hot tortillas and serve immediately.

Note: Hot pitta bread can be served in place of the tortillas.

Serves 6

Chicken and Tomato Croissants

Croissants are now readily available both fresh and frozen. Keep some on hand to create an easy snack.

30 g butter
3 shallots (spring onions, scallions), chopped
2 chicken breast fillets, chopped
1 stick celery, chopped
2 tomatoes, chopped
60 g mushrooms, sliced
salt and pepper to taste
3 tablespoons cornflour
2 cups milk
1 tablespoon finely chopped parsley
4 croissants
parsley to garnish

Melt the butter in a saucepan and gently fry the shallots until soft and transparent, then add the chicken and celery. Cook until the chicken turns opaque. Add the tomatoes and mushrooms and season with salt and pepper.

Mix the cornflour and milk together until smooth, then add to the chicken. Stir in the parsley and cook until thickened, stirring constantly.

Heat the croissants in an oven preheated to 190°C (375°F) for 5 minutes. Slice the croissants and put the base onto serving plates. Spoon the chicken mixture over and top with the remaining croissant half. Serve garnished with parsley.

Serves 4

Tomato and Olive Savoury

1 tablespoon oil
2 onions, finely chopped
3 rashers bacon, rind removed, finely chopped
8 small tomatoes, quartered
1 tablespoon flour
2 tablespoons white wine
8 black olives, pitted and finely chopped
20 g butter
salt and pepper, to taste

Heat the oil in a pan and gently fry the onions until golden brown, then fry the bacon until crisp. Mix in the tomatoes and simmer for 5 minutes or until softened. Stir in the flour and cook for 2 minutes until the flour is lightly browned, stirring constantly.

Blend in the wine and olives, reduce the heat and simmer for a few minutes or until thickened. Stir in the butter and season to taste with salt and pepper. Serve immediately on toast or on a bed of rice or pasta.

Serves 4

Chilli Tomatoes

500 g tomatoes, cored, peeled and chopped
1 tablespoon onion flakes
1 clove garlic, crushed
125 g can chopped green chillies
1 cup White Sauce (see recipe)
1 cup grated tasty cheese

Place the tomatoes, onion, garlic and chillies into a saucepan and simmer for 15 minutes or until the tomatoes are soft and pulpy. Stir in the White Sauce and season with salt.

Just before serving, stir in the cheese. Serve in bowls with chunks of crusty bread.

Serves 6–8

Tomato Pikelets

750 g tomatoes, cored, peeled and chopped
4 eggs
1 cup flour
1 cup dried breadcrumbs
60 g butter, melted
1 tablespoon finely chopped parsley
½ teaspoon dried mixed herbs
2 teaspoons Worcestershire sauce
salt and pepper, to taste

Put the tomatoes into a heavy-based pan and simmer over low heat until pulpy. This may be done in a microwave-safe bowl in the microwave oven. Cover and cook on high for 5 minutes. Set aside and cool.

Beat the eggs until slightly thickened, then stir in the flour, breadcrumbs, butter, herbs and Worcestershire sauce. Season to taste. Add the tomatoes to the egg mixture, stirring until well blended. Drop tablespoonsful of the mixture onto a hot, greased frying pan. Cook for 1–2 minutes or until browned on the bottom then turn over and brown on the other side.

Serve immediately.

Serves 4

Savoury Pancake Parcel (front), Tomato Pikelets

Hot Turkey and Tomato Sandwiches

Hot Turkey and Tomato Sandwiches

100 g butter
¼ cup flour
2 cups milk
salt and pepper, to taste
2 egg yolks
2–3 drops Tabasco sauce
2 tablespoons grated tasty
  cheese

2 tablespoons cream
4 slices bread
4 slices white turkey meat
4 slices tomato
4 bacon rashers, partially
  cooked, rind removed
2 tablespoons grated
  Parmesan cheese

Melt 60 g butter in a heavy-based pan, stir in the flour and cook for 1 minute or until foaming but not brown. Gradually whisk in the milk, stirring constantly. Cook until the sauce is boiling, stirring until thickened.

Blend 40 g butter into the white sauce, then beat in the egg yolks and Tabasco. Stir in the cheese and cream. Keep warm by covering the sauce closely with waxed paper and placing over a very low heat.

Toast the bread on one side only, then top the untoasted side with the turkey, tomato, white sauce and bacon.

Sprinkle over the Parmesan cheese and grill until the cheese is brown and bubbling.

Variations: Ham, chicken or sliced cold sausage meat may be substituted for the turkey.

Serves 4

Curd Recipes

When an acid is added to boiled milk, two products are formed, curds and whey. The curd is used in many vegetarian preparations, including sweets. Whey can be mixed with equal quantities of fruit juice, sweetened with honey or sugar and served chilled as a refreshing drink.

For every litre of milk, you require:

¾–1 cup natural yoghurt
  or
3 teaspoons of lemon juice,
  strained
  or
1 teaspoon citric acid (added
  gradually)

Bring the milk to the boil, then add the curdling agent. Reduce heat and simmer the mixture for a few minutes, after which the solids will rise to the top.

Transfer the solids with a slotted spoon to a colander or sieve and allow the excess whey to drain off. Place an inverted plate on top and weight with a can of food. Leave for 15 minutes to set.

The curd can be cut into cubes and fried, crumbled like cottage cheese, or coated in breadcrumbs, rolled into balls and fried for use in salads, rices or vegetable curries.

Fried Curd Balls with Tomato, Eggplant and Potatoes

Asafoetida, used here, is a plant extract made from ferula stems. It is quite strong and salty, so use sparingly. Usually sold as a powder or in small pieces from Asian food stores it is quite useful in vegetarian cookery.

curd from 3 litres of milk (see recipe)
ghee, for deep frying
3 large potatoes
3 eggplants (aubergines)
1 teaspoon cumin seeds
4 chillies, chopped
½ teaspoon asafoetida
½ teaspoon turmeric
¼ teaspoon ground coriander
12 tomatoes, pureed
1 teaspoon salt

Press the curd, then knead until soft. Roll into 1.5 cm balls. Heat enough ghee to cover the balls and deep fry until golden. Drain on absorbent paper.

Cut the potato and eggplant into 2.5 cm cubes. Fry the potatoes in the ghee, then drain on absorbent paper.

Drain the ghee, leaving 1 tablespoon in the pan, then add the cumin seeds, chillies, asafoetida, turmeric, coriander and tomato puree. Season with the salt and stir in the eggplant cubes. Simmer for 20 minutes or until eggplant is soft. Fold in the curd balls and potatoes and continue simmering until heated through. Serve with rice.

Serves 6–8

1 Scoop off solids with a slotted spoon and transfer to a sieve placed over a glass bowl

2 Place an inverted plate over the top and weight with a can until set

Oeufs en Cocotte

This dish can be served at any meal during the day, from breakfast through to supper.

6 large tomatoes, cored and peeled
30–45 g butter
500 g button mushrooms, thickly sliced
pinch basil
pinch sugar

8 eggs
salt and pepper, to taste
1 cup grated tasty cheese
1 green capsicum (pepper), seeded and cut into fine strips

Cut the tomatoes into 2.5 cm cubes and drain well. Melt the butter in a large frying pan and gently fry the mushrooms for 3–4 minutes. Add the tomatoes, basil and sugar and simmer for 30 minutes or until the sauce has thickened.

Using a tablespoon, make 8 indents into the tomato mixture and break an egg into each. Season with salt and pepper and sprinkle over the cheese and capsicum strips. Cover the pan and cook gently until the eggs have set.

Serves 4

Fried Curd with Peas and Tomatoes

8 large, ripe tomatoes, cored and peeled
curd from 2 litres of milk (see recipe)
1 tablespoon ghee
1 teaspoon cumin seeds
2 small chillies, chopped
1 teaspoon salt

1 tablespoon paprika
1 teaspoon ground coriander
1 tablespoon brown sugar
500 g shelled peas, or frozen peas, thawed
2 tablespoons chopped fresh coriander, to garnish

Cut the tomatoes into eighths and the curd into 2.5 cm cubes. Heat the ghee in a pan and fry the cumin seeds and chillies until brown, then add the tomatoes, salt, paprika, ground coriander, brown sugar and peas. Cook, covered, over a medium heat for 10 minutes.

Add the curd cubes and stir, then simmer for 5 minutes. Sprinkle with the fresh coriander and serve with rice.

Serves 4

1 Add the tomatoes and basil to fried mushrooms

2 Carefully break an egg into each indent in the tomato mixture

3 Sprinkle over the capsicum strips and cheese

Spanish Omelette

2 red capsicums (peppers), seeded and cut into thin strips
40 g butter
1 small onion, chopped
2 cloves garlic, crushed
250 g tomatoes, cored, peeled and chopped
4 eggs
3 tablespoons milk
¼ teaspoon oregano
salt and pepper, to taste

Blanch the capsicums in boiling salted water for 5 minutes, then drain. Heat the butter in an omelette pan and fry the onion and garlic until soft but not browned. Add the capsicum and tomatoes and cook for a further 5–10 minutes, until all the vegetables are tender.

Beat together the eggs and milk then season with oregano and salt and pepper to taste. Pour the egg mixture over vegetables, tilting the pan to spread the omelette evenly. Cook over low heat until the eggs have just set, then place the pan under a hot grill for 1–2 minutes or until top has set. Serve immediately.

Serves 2–3

Tomato and Gruyere Quiche

Quiches are always superb for picnics or light luncheons, especially if served with crisp green salad, olives and chilled white wine.

750 g firm ripe tomatoes, cored, peeled and chopped
1 x 375 g packet frozen puff pastry, thawed
90 g Gruyere cheese, grated
½ cup cream
2 eggs
salt and pepper, to taste
pinch basil

Preheat oven to 230°C (450°F). Place a baking tray in the oven to heat. Drain the tomatoes in a colander and season. Roll out the pastry thinly to line a 23 cm flan tin, then sprinkle over a third of the grated cheese.

Beat the cream, eggs and seasonings together. Spoon the tomatoes into the pastry case, spreading them out evenly, then pour in the egg mixture. Pastry off-cuts can be cut into strips and used to give a lattice top to the quiche.

Place the quiche onto the preheated oven tray and bake for 5 minutes. Reduce the temperature to 200°C (400°F) and bake for a further 5 minutes. Lower the temperature to 180°C (360°F) and continue baking for another 30 minutes, or until the filling is puffed and golden. If the pastry browns before the filling has set, cover the top with a 30 cm circle of aluminium foil.

Serves 4–6

Tomato Omelette

30 g butter
2 tablespoons chopped parsley
¼ cup finely chopped onion
500 g tomatoes, cored, peeled and chopped
salt and pepper, to taste
6 eggs
Fresh Tomato Sauce (see recipe), for serving

Melt half the butter in a pan and add half the parsley and the onion. Fry gently for a few minutes, then add the tomatoes. Season to taste with salt and pepper. Cook, uncovered, for 30 minutes or until the mixture has thickened.

Break the eggs into a bowl and whisk until thoroughly combined.

Melt the remaining butter in a pan until foaming but not brown. Add one quarter of the eggs and cook over low heat moving the mixture with a fork until lightly set. Fold the omelette in half and remove from the pan. Make an incision down the centre and fill it with the hot tomato mixture. Make three more omelettes in the same way. Sprinkle with the remaining parsley. Serve with Fresh Tomato Sauce.

Serves 4

Cheese Omelette with Tomato Mushroom Sauce

6 eggs
½ cup cream
pinch cayenne pepper
½ cup grated tasty cheese
60 g butter

Tomato Mushroom Sauce
15 g butter
3 shallots (spring onions, scallions), chopped
125 g mushrooms, chopped
2 tomatoes, cored, peeled and chopped
¼ cup sour (dairy soured) cream

Whisk the eggs with the cream until fluffy. Season with cayenne pepper, then fold in the cheese.

Grease an omelette pan with butter. Heat the pan, then pour in a quarter of the omelette mix. Cook over low heat until just set then fold the omelette in half. Continue cooking until the egg has set and the omelette is brown. Cook the remaining omelettes.

To make the sauce, melt the butter in a saucepan and gently fry the shallots. Add the mushrooms and tomatoes and cook for 20 minutes or until the mixture reduces to pulp. Add the sour cream and cook for 1 minute more.

Place the omelettes onto entree plates and serve topped with sauce.

Serves 4

Spanish Omelette (front), Tomato Omelette

1 Using fingertips rub the butter into the flour

2 Gradually stir in the water and egg yolk using a knife

3 Lightly knead the dough to form a smooth ball

4 Roll out the dough onto a lightly floured surface

Onion and Blue Cheese Quiche

Pastry
2 cups flour
salt
125 g butter
1 egg yolk
cold water

Filling
2 tablespoons oil
1 onion, chopped
1 clove garlic, crushed
3 tomatoes, chopped
1 teaspoon oregano
freshly ground black pepper
3 eggs, beaten

90 g blue vein cheese, crumbled
¼ cup grated Parmesan cheese
4–6 lettuce leaves and cherry tomatoes, to garnish

To make the pastry, sift flour and salt into a bowl, then rub in the butter until the mixture resembles breadcrumbs. Add the egg and just enough water to form a firm dough. Knead quickly on a floured board until the pastry is smooth. Cover and leave in the refrigerator for 20 minutes.

Meanwhile, heat the oil in a saucepan and fry the onion and garlic until soft and transparent. Mix in the tomatoes, oregano, pepper, eggs and blue vein cheese.

Roll the pastry out to a 6 mm thickness and cut to fit 4–6 individual quiche dishes. Bake blind in an oven preheated to 200°C (400°F) for 10 minutes. Pour mixture into pastry cases. Bake for 10 minutes, then sprinkle over the Parmesan cheese. Continue cooking at 180°C (350°F) for 20–30 minutes more or until the top is golden and set. Serve garnished with lettuce and cherry tomatoes.

Serves 4–6

Cheese and Tomato Flan

1 sheet ready-rolled short-crust pastry
6 bacon rashers, rind removed
1 tomato
1 cup grated tasty cheese
3 eggs
1¾ cups milk
¼ cup chopped parsley
salt and pepper, to taste

Line a 23 cm plate with the prepared pastry. Fry the bacon until crisp, then crumble into small pieces. Cut the tomato into 8 wedges and arrange them in a circle on the pie shell. Sprinkle with the crumbed bacon and cheese.

Blend the eggs, milk and parsley together. Season to taste with salt and pepper, then pour over the tomato. Bake in an oven preheated to 180°C (350°F) for 50 minutes or until the custard has set and the pastry is brown. Allow the flan to stand for 20 minutes before serving.

Serves 4–6

Tomato and Anchovy Flan

250 g pastry (see Onion and Blue Cheese Quiche recipe)
175 g Cheddar cheese, grated
2 eggs, lightly beaten
1 tablespoon flour
1 cup milk
salt and freshly ground pepper
2 tomatoes, skinned and sliced
30 g butter
8 anchovy fillets

Roll out the pastry and line a 23 cm flan dish. Bake pastry blind for 15 minutes at 190°C (375°F). Remove and cool slightly.

Combine the cheese, eggs, flour and sufficient milk to make a soft paste. Spread over the base of the pastry case and season with salt and pepper. Arrange the tomatoes over the filling in an overlapping pattern. Dot with butter and bake at 180°C (350°F) for 20–30 minutes or until the filling has set. Garnish with anchovies.

Serves 4

Onion and Blue Cheese Quiche

Scalloped Potatoes and Tomatoes

Tomato and Chick Pea Subji

10 medium-sized tomatoes,
    cored, peeled and chopped
1 tablespoon ghee
1 teaspoon cumin seeds
4–6 small chillies, chopped
¼ teaspoon asafoetida
1 teaspoon ground coriander
1 teaspoon turmeric
2 teaspoons paprika
1½ teaspoons salt

6 medium-sized zucchini
    (courgettes), cut into
    2.5 cm pieces
3 large capsicum (pepper),
    seeded and cut into 2.5 cm
    pieces
400 g can chick peas
    (garbanzo beans), drained
2 teaspoons brown sugar
½ tablespoon fresh basil or
    ½ teaspoon dried basil

Put the tomatoes into a large saucepan, bring to the boil, then simmer, uncovered, until tender.

Heat the ghee in a pan, add the cumin seeds and chillies. Fry until brown. Stir in the asafoetida, coriander and turmeric, and cook until brown, then blend the spice mixture into the tomato puree. Season with the paprika and salt.

Stir in the zucchini and capsicum and simmer until soft. Add the chick peas, brown sugar and basil and simmer for a further 10 minutes, adding a little whey or vegetable stock if more liquid is required.

Serve with rice or pasta.

Serves 4

Scalloped Potatoes and Tomatoes

3 tablespoons olive oil
2 onions, finely sliced
750 g tomatoes, chopped
2–3 cloves garlic, chopped
1 teaspoon chopped fresh
    basil
1 teaspoon chopped fresh
    thyme
1 tablespoon chopped
    parsley
salt and pepper, to taste
1 kg potatoes, finely sliced
2 tablespoons grated cheese

Heat one tablespoon of the oil and fry the onions until soft, then add the tomatoes and heat through. Combine the garlic and herbs with salt and pepper to taste and one tablespoon of the oil.

Lightly grease a baking dish and spread over one third of the tomato mixture. Cover with half the potato, arranged in overlapping slices. Layer the remaining tomato mixture, garlic mixture and potatoes, finishing with a layer of tomato. Sprinkle with the cheese and remaining oil.

Bake in an oven preheated to 200°C (400°F) for 45 minutes or until the potatoes are tender.
Variation: If serving as an accompaniment to lamb, omit the basil and substitute rosemary.

Serves 6

Cauliflower Koftas in Tomato Sauce

12 large, ripe or cooking
    tomatoes, pureed
1 tablespoon brown sugar
1 bay leaf
1 teaspoon salt

1 tablespoon paprika
30 g butter
1 teaspoon basil
ghee, for deep frying

Koftas

1½ large cauliflowers
¾ cup chick pea flour (also
    called Besan flour)
1 teaspoon cumin
1 teaspoon coriander
2–3 teaspoons salt
1 teaspoon turmeric

¼ teaspoon asafoetida
¼ teaspoon ginger powder
½ teaspoon fenugreek
    powder
¼ teaspoon cayenne pepper
1 egg, lightly beaten

Pour the tomato puree into a saucepan and bring it to the boil. Add the brown sugar, bay leaf, salt, paprika, butter and basil then simmer, uncovered, until the mixture thickens. Keep warm until required.

Meanwhile, to make the koftas, grate the cauliflower finely, then add the chick pea flour, all the spices and egg. Mix well. Heat the ghee in a deep, straight-sided pan. Squeeze the cauliflower mixture into walnut-sized balls, then fry small batches in the hot ghee until firm and dark brown. Remove from the ghee, drain on absorbent paper, and arrange on serving plate.

Pour the hot tomato sauce over the koftas allowing them to soak for a few minutes before serving.
Note: Do not grate the cauliflower until ready to use as it will become very moist.

Serves 6–8

Cauliflower Koftas in Tomato Sauce

Prawn and Egg Curry

20 g butter
1 small onion, chopped
2 cloves garlic, crushed
1–2 teaspoons curry powder
¼ teaspoon chilli powder
¼ cup water
250 g tomatoes, cored,
   peeled and chopped
½ cup chicken stock
750 g uncooked prawns,
   shelled
4 hard-boiled eggs, quartered
salt, to taste
½ teaspoon lemon juice

Melt the butter in a heavy based pan and gently fry the onion and garlic until soft but not browned. Blend the curry and chilli powder with the water and stir into onion and garlic. Add the tomatoes and simmer over low heat for 5 minutes, stirring constantly.

Pour in the stock, add the prawns and simmer for 2–3 minutes or until the prawns are opaque and cooked. Mix in the eggs, salt to taste and lemon juice. Combine, simmering until heated through. Serve with rice.

Serves 4

Crab and Prawn Creole

1 tablespoon oil
20 g butter
¼ cup chopped green
   capsicum (pepper)
¼ cup chopped onion
3 cups cooked rice
200 g can shelled
   prawns, chopped
200 g can crabmeat,
   drained and flaked
180 g tasty cheese, diced
¾ cup white wine
½ cup chopped tomatoes
freshly ground black pepper
cayenne pepper
dash Tabasco sauce, to taste
lemon slices and parsley
   sprigs, to garnish

Heat the oil and butter in a heavy-based pan, gently fry the capsicum and onion until soft but not browned. Stir in the rice, mixing well until well coated with the oil and butter. Mix in the prawns, crabmeat and cheese and cook, stirring until the cheese has melted.

Blend in the wine and tomatoes, and season to taste with salt, cayenne, pepper and Tabasco sauce. Simmer over low heat, stirring constantly for 5–10 minutes or until the mixture has thickened slightly.

Spoon into a heated serving dish and garnish with lemon and parsley. Serve with a tossed green salad.

Serves 6–8

Nutmeat Ratatouille

1 x 440 g canned nutmeat
250 g eggplant (aubergine)
250 g zucchini (courgettes)
250 g ripe tomatoes, peeled,
   seeded and chopped
2 tablespoons oil
1 medium-sized onion
1 clove garlic, chopped
1 teaspoon sugar
pinch basil
salt and pepper to taste
1 tablespoon chopped
   parsley

Cut the nutmeat into 2.5 cm cubes. Trim both ends of the eggplant and zucchini and cut into 2.5 cm cubes.

Heat the oil in a saucepan and gently fry the onions for 7 minutes. Add the garlic, eggplant and zucchini cubes, season with the sugar, basil, salt and pepper and simmer, covered, for another 5 minutes. Add the tomatoes and continue cooking over low heat for 20 minutes.

Stir in the nutmeat cubes and cook for a further 10 minutes. Taste and adjust the seasoning if necessary. Stir in the parsley. Serve with pasta or rice.

Serves 4–6

Chicken Liver Snack

Chicken livers are easy to prepare and have a wonderful flavour if handled correctly. Always rinse livers with cold water and discard any that may be coloured slightly green as these are very bitter to eat.

40 g butter
1 small onion, finely chopped
1 tomato, cored, peeled and
   chopped
4 mushrooms, chopped
¼ teaspoon dried rosemary
salt and pepper, to taste
125 g chicken livers, cleaned
   and chopped

Melt 25 g of the butter in a pan and gently fry the onion for 5 minutes or until soft but not browned. Add the tomato, mushrooms and rosemary and season to taste with salt and pepper. Cook for 3 minutes, then push the vegetables to one side. Melt the remaining butter, then add the chicken livers. Cook for 4 minutes, stirring occasionally. Serve on toast.

Serves 2–4

Prawn and Egg Curry

Arabian Mixed Vegetables

(Chop the vegetables into bite-sized pieces in this delicious recipe.)

2 tablespoons oil
1 small onion, finely chopped
½ bay leaf
¾ teaspoon mustard seeds
½ teaspoon dried dill
¼ teaspoon celery seeds
1 potato, peeled and
    chopped
1 carrot, peeled and chopped
500 g cauliflower, chopped
1 Granny Smith apple, cored
    and chopped
2 tomatoes, cored, peeled
    and chopped
2 small zucchini (courgettes),
    chopped
½ teaspoon paprika

Heat the oil in a large, heavy based pan and gently fry the onion, spices and herbs for 10 minutes until the onion is soft but not browned. Stir in the potato, carrot, cauliflower, apple, tomatoes and zucchini, allowing 2 minutes between each addition.

Simmer for 20 minutes or until the vegetables are tender. Season to taste with paprika.

Serves 4–6

Arabian Mixed Vegetables

Beans Provencale

⅓ cup olive oil
2 onions, finely sliced
6 tomatoes
3 cloves garlic, crushed
bouquet garni
salt and pepper, to taste
1 kg green beans, topped and
    tailed, blanched
2 tablespoons chopped
    parsley, to garnish

Heat the oil in a large pan. Add the onions and cook over a gentle heat until soft, about 10 minutes.

Peel and core the tomatoes and remove the seeds. Sieve the seeds and reserve the juice. Make the juice up to 150 mL with water. Chop the tomatoes. Add the tomatoes, garlic, bouquet garni and tomato liquid to the onions and season with salt and pepper. Bring to the boil then reduce the heat and simmer for 30 minutes.

Add the beans to the pan, cover and simmer for 10 minutes or until the beans are tender. Serve, sprinkled with the parsley.

Micro Method

Place the oil in a large microwave-safe casserole dish, add the onions, then cover and cook on high for 3 minutes. Add the prepared tomatoes, garlic, bouquet garni, tomato liquid and seasoning. Cover and cook on high for 10 minutes.

Add the beans and turn through the sauce to coat. Cook a further 10 minutes on high or until the beans are tender. Sprinkle with parsley.

Serves 6–8

Italian Vegetable Hotpot

1 medium-sized cauliflower
3 tablespoons oil
1 onion, finely chopped
1 clove garlic, crushed
1 small green capsicum
    (pepper), chopped
6 tomatoes, cored, peeled
    and roughly chopped
salt and pepper, to taste
1 tablespoon chopped
    parsley and
1 teaspoon capers, chopped,
    to garnish

Cut the cauliflower into florets, discarding the thick white stalk. Wash and shake off the excess water.

Heat the oil in a frying pan, add the onion and garlic and cook until the onion is soft and translucent. Add the cauliflower, cover and cook over a gentle heat for 10 minutes, stirring occasionally. Stir in the capsicum, tomatoes and salt and pepper to taste. Cover and heat through. Combine the parsley and capers and sprinkle over the top.

Serves 4–6

Italian Vegetable Hotpot

Sweet and Sour Vegetables in Tomato Sauce

To keep herbs and spices fresh, always store in well sealed jars away from direct sunlight. Never store two or more in the same jar as flavours will lose their personality.

10 large, ripe tomatoes,
    cored, peeled and chopped
2 tablespoons ghee
1 teaspoon cumin seeds
2–3 red chillies, chopped
1 teaspoon fenugreek seeds
¼ teaspoon anise seeds
1 teaspoon ginger powder
1 teaspoon turmeric
1 teaspoon salt
¼ cup white apple cider
    vinegar, or
    ½ cup lemon juice,
    strained
1 cup brown sugar
¼ cup cornflour

½ cup water
curd from 2 litres milk (see
    recipe), whey reserved
1 small pineapple, cut into
    2.5 cm cubes
1 red capsicum (pepper), cut
    into 2.5 cm cubes
1 green capsicum (pepper),
    cut into 2.5 cm cubes
3 carrots, cut into strips
3 sticks celery, cut into strips
½ cup bamboo shoots, sliced
½ cup water chestnuts, sliced
2 cups bean sprouts
¾ cup cashew nuts, roasted
ghee, for deep frying

Put the tomatoes into a large saucepan and bring to the boil. Simmer, uncovered, until tender.

Heat the ghee in a wok, add the cumin seeds and chillies, and fry until brown. Stir in the fenugreek and anise and cook until browned. Reduce the heat and add the ginger, turmeric and salt, blending well.

Stir the vinegar and brown sugar into the tomato puree. Blend the cornflour with the water mixing until smooth, then whisk it into the sauce, stirring until thickened.

Cut the curd into 2.5 cm cubes and deep fry in the ghee. When golden, soak in the whey until required.

Reheat the wok and add 2 tablespoons of ghee, then fry the remaining ingredients in the following order: pineapple, red and green capsicum, carrot, celery, bamboo shoots, water chestnuts and bean sprouts. Cook until crisp but tender.

Drain the curd and add it to the tomato sauce, then mix in the vegetables, simmering the mixture for a few minutes. Top with cashew nuts and serve with rice.

Serves 6–8

Sweet and Sour Vegetables in Tomato Sauce

Okra, Corn and Tomato Melange

Colourful vegetables cooked in Cajun style.

4 rashers bacon, rind
   removed
200 g fresh or canned okra,
   cut into 5 mm slices
1 onion, finely chopped
220 g can corn kernels,
   drained

3 large tomatoes, cored,
   peeled and chopped
1 small green capsicum
   (pepper), seeded and
   chopped
salt and pepper, to taste
2–4 drops Tabasco sauce

Fry the bacon until crisp, then drain on absorbent paper and crumble. Set aside.

Stir the okra and onion into the bacon fat and cook for a few minutes, then add the corn and cook for 10 minutes, stirring constantly. Stir in the tomatoes and capsicum and season to taste with salt, pepper and Tabasco.

Cover the pot and simmer for 25 minutes or until the vegetables are tender. Pour the mixture into a heated serving dish and sprinkle over the bacon.

Serves 6

Braised Zucchini and Tomatoes

A simple dish for grilled or barbecued meat

750 g zucchini, topped and
   tailed
80 g butter
3 tomatoes, cored, peeled
   and chopped
salt and pepper, to taste
1 tablespoon chopped fresh
   dill

Shred the zucchini, heat the butter in a pan, and cook the zucchini over a low heat for 5 minutes, stirring occasionally. Add the tomatoes and season with salt and pepper. Cover the pan and simmer for a further 5 minutes, then spoon the mixture into a serving dish and sprinkle over the dill.

Serves 6

1 Remove stem end from zucchini. Cut lengthways into thin slices

2 Shred the remaining zucchini

Ratatouille

The flavour of this dish will develop and improve on keeping. Prepare and store in the refrigerator overnight. Ratatouille may be served warm or chilled.

3 medium-sized eggplants
   (aubergine)
salt and pepper, to taste
½ cup olive oil
3 onions, finely sliced
3–4 cloves garlic, crushed
500 g zucchini (courgettes),
   sliced diagonally
500 g tomatoes, sliced thickly
3 green capsicums (peppers),
   cored, seeded and sliced

Cut the eggplant into 1 cm slices. Sprinkle with salt and leave for 30 minutes. Rinse and pat dry.

Heat half the oil in a heavy based saucepan, add the onions and garlic and cook until the onion is soft. Add the eggplant and zucchini and fry, in batches, for three minutes each side, adding extra oil if necessary. Return the fried eggplant to the pan and season with pepper. Add the capsicum and tomatoes and season with more pepper. Cover the pan and simmer for 45 minutes or until the ratatouille is very soft.

Serves 8

Braised Zucchini and Tomatoes

Individual Duck and Tomato Pies

Delicious golden baked puff pastry is used as a topping for these pies filled with an unusual duck and tomato combination.

2 tablespoons oil
1.5 kg duck meat, cut into
  2.5 cm cubes
250 g button mushrooms
2 stalks celery, sliced
1 onion, sliced
1 teaspoon oregano
freshly ground black pepper
2 cups white wine

1 cup tomatoes, cored,
  peeled and chopped
3 tablespoons cornflour
3 tablespoons water
1 chicken stock cube
1 egg yolk
extra ½ tablespoon water
1 packet frozen puff pastry,
  thawed
3 tablespoons poppy seeds

Heat the oil in a large frying pan, add the duck and cook until browned. Stir in the mushrooms, celery, onion, oregano, pepper, white wine and tomato. Cover the pan and bring to the boil, then simmer for 1 hour. Combine the cornflour, water and stock cube, mixing until smooth. Whisk this into the duck mixture, stirring until thickened. Boil for 2 minutes stirring continually. Spoon into 6 x 2-cup souffle or similar dishes.

Mix the egg yolk with the water and set aside. Roll out the pastry, then cut into 6 rounds large enough to fit the tops of individual souffle dishes. Brush the edge of the dishes with the egg and water mixture. Top with pastry and press down the edges to secure.

Using the remaining pastry, cut 5 cm long triangles and roll them sideways to form a rose. Glaze the roses with the egg and water, then place on top of the pies. Cut a 2.5 cm slit in the tops and glaze each pie, then sprinkle over the poppy seeds. Bake the pies in an oven preheated to 220°C (425°)F for 15 minutes or until golden brown.

Serves 6

Eggplant and Tomato Pie

This lovely vegetarian dish can be prepared in advance and then baked when required.

1 kg small to medium-sized
  eggplant (aubergine), sliced
salt and pepper, to taste
flour, seasoned with salt and
  pepper
½ cup olive oil

375 g mozzarella cheese,
  sliced
¾ cup Fresh Tomato Sauce
  (see recipe)
½ cup freshly grated
  Parmesan cheese

Sprinkle the eggplant with the salt and leave for 30 minutes. Dust the slices with seasoned flour. Heat half the oil in a frying pan and fry the eggplant, in batches, until softened, adding more oil to the pan if necessary. Drain the eggplant on paper towels.

Lightly grease a deep cake tin, about 18–20 cm in diameter. Make layers of eggplant, mozzarella and Tomato Sauce, starting with eggplant and finishing with Tomato Sauce and seasoning each layer with salt and pepper. Top with the Parmesan cheese then bake in an oven preheated to 180°C (350°F) for 30 minutes. Serve hot, cut into wedges.

Serves 6–8

Grilled Tomatoes with Basil Butter

Basil Butter can be frozen successfully. Keep some handy for barbecued meats, herb bread or baked potatoes.

6 tomatoes
salt and pepper, to taste

Basil Butter

90 g butter, softened
1 clove garlic, crushed
2 tablespoons chopped fresh
  basil

1 tablespoon chopped
  parsley
good squeeze lemon juice

1 Place the freshly creamed Basil Butter onto a sheet of aluminium foil

2 Using a metal spatula, roll the butter into a log shape, wrapping the aluminium foil around it

3 Twist the ends tightly to seal and freeze until firm

To prepare the butter, beat until soft, add the remaining ingredients and season to taste with salt and pepper. Stir well until the ingredients are well blended, turn onto a piece of aluminium foil and form into a log shape. Seal well and freeze until firm.

Vandyke the tomatoes (see illustration page 10). Preheat the grill and lightly brush the tomatoes with oil. Place the tomatoes, cut side down, on the grill tray and grill for 3–5 minutes. Turn, season with salt and pepper and grill for a further 3–5 minutes.

Cut the butter into 12 slices. Place one slice of butter on each tomato and serve hot.

Serves 6

Grilled Tomatoes with Basil Butter

STUFFED VEGETABLES

Firm, round tomatoes make colourful containers for a variety of fillings. They can be served on their own as a course or snack or arranged on a serving platter for a decorative touch to the dinner table.

To prepare, halve the tomatoes and scoop out the seeds and membranes with a teaspoon. If using cherry tomatoes, leave whole, slice off the top and remove pulp. Drain tomato shells while preparing the filling. Pat shells dry with absorbent paper before filling.

Tomatoes with Rice

This recipe uses Basmati rice, which is tender and fluffy when cooked, without breaking up.

6 tomatoes
2 tablespoons olive oil
1 small onion, finely chopped
¾ cup Basmati rice, washed
1½ cups chicken stock
2 tablespoons sultanas
1 small green capsicum
    (pepper), seeded and
    chopped
salt and pepper, to taste
3 lemons
extra ¼ cup olive oil

Slice the top off the tomatoes and scoop out the seeds and membranes.

Heat the oil, add the onion and cook until soft, then mix in the rice and stir until coated with the oil. Add the chicken stock and bring to the boil. Stir in the sultanas. Cover the pan and simmer until the rice is tender and the liquid has been absorbed. Stir in the capsicum, then season with salt and pepper.

Fill the tomatoes with the rice mixture and place in a pan small enough to hold them upright. Squeeze the juice of two of the lemons and combine with the oil. Pour around the tomatoes along with enough water to come halfway up the sides. Cover the pan and gently simmer the tomatoes for 30 minutes, then leave to cool in the pan. Lift from liquid and set aside. Serve the cooled or chilled tomatoes garnished with the remaining lemon, sliced.

Serves 6

Savoury Fillings for Tomatoes

Green Cheese Filling

500 g ricotta cheese
½ green capsicum (pepper),
    seeded and finely chopped
¼ teaspoon finely chopped
    fresh basil or pinch of
    dried basil
salt and pepper, to taste

Mix ingredients together, season and fill the tomato shells.

Makes 12

Cheese and Bacon Filling

4 bacon rashers, rinds
    removed
500 g cream cheese
salt and pepper, to taste

Fry bacon until crisp, finely chop and when cool, mix into the cream cheese. Season with salt and pepper and spoon into the tomato shells.

Makes 12

Curry Mushroom Filling

12 large mushrooms, chopped	1 cup sour (dairy soured) cream
12 artichoke hearts, quartered	2 teaspoons curry powder
1 cup oil and vinegar dressing	2 teaspoons lemon juice
2 cups mayonnaise	2 teaspoons grated onion
	lettuce leaves and sprigs of dill, to garnish

Marinate the mushrooms and artichokes in the oil and vinegar dressing for 6 hours or overnight.

Combine the mayonnaise with the sour cream, then stir in the curry powder, lemon juice and onion. Drain the mushrooms and artichokes, and mix into the mayonnaise dressing.

Spoon the mixture into the tomato shells, arrange on lettuce leaves and garnish each with a sprig of dill.

Makes 6

Tomatoes with Rice

Herbed Filling

Fresh herbs bring out the flavour of sun-ripened tomatoes. These savoury tomatoes add colour and zest to the family baked dinner.

6 large tomatoes
¼ cup finely chopped parsley
4 tablespoons finely chopped
    fresh basil
1 teaspoon finely chopped
    fresh thyme
3 tablespoons chopped
    shallots (spring onions,
    scallions)
3 cloves garlic, crushed
salt and pepper, to taste
¼–½ cup fresh breadcrumbs
oil
lemon wedges, to garnish

Prepare the tomatoes, reserving the pulp. Combine the pulp with the herbs, shallots and garlic. Season to taste, then bind with sufficient breadcrumbs to make a thick paste. Spoon the mixture into each tomato shell and brush with the oil.

Arrange the tomatoes in an oiled, shallow ovenproof dish and cover with an oiled lid. Bake in an oven preheated to 180°C (350°F) for 30 minutes. Remove the lid, increase the heat to 200°C (400°F) and bake for a further 5 minutes. Serve garnished with the lemon wedges.

Serves 4–6

Cheese and Mushroom Stuffing

10 medium-sized tomatoes
60 g butter
¼ cup oil
12 shallots (spring onions,
    scallions), chopped
2 cloves garlic, crushed
2 teaspoons oregano
½ teaspoon thyme
½ teaspoon basil
2 bay leaves
⅓ teaspoon chilli powder
220 g can mushroom
    pieces
1 cup fresh breadcrumbs
½ cup grated Parmesan
    cheese

Prepare the tomatoes, reserving the pulp. Heat the butter and oil in a pan and gently fry the shallots and garlic until soft. Add the herbs, chilli powder and mushrooms with the liquid and cook for 5 minutes. Mix in the tomato pulp, then simmer for 20–30 minutes. Remove the bay leaves. Add the breadcrumbs and cheese and stir well.

Spoon the mixture into each tomato shell and sprinkle with extra cheese, if desired. Arrange in an oiled, shallow ovenproof dish and bake in an oven preheated to 180°C (350°F) for 30 minutes or until the tomatoes are tender.

Serves 5

Cheese Souffle Filling

8 medium-sized tomatoes
40 g butter
1 tablespoon flour
1 teaspoon curry powder
salt and pepper, to taste
1 cup grated cheese
3 eggs, separated

Prepare the tomatoes and set aside. Melt the butter in a shallow pan and add the flour, curry powder and salt and pepper. Cook for 1 minute (or microwave). Beat in the cheese until well blended, remove from heat then mix in the egg yolks.

Beat the egg whites until stiff peaks form, then fold gently into the mixture. Spoon the souffle into the tomato shells until each one is three-quarters full. Arrange in a greased shallow ovenproof dish and bake in an oven preheated to 180°C (350°F) for 15 minutes. Serve immediately.

Serves 4

Curry and Rice Combination

4 large tomatoes
1 packet Dutch Curry and
    Rice Soup
2 cups water
250 g uncooked prawns, shelled
1 cup cooked rice

Prepare the tomatoes, and set aside. Make up the soup with the water, stir in the prawns and rice and mix well. Spoon the mixture into each shell and bake in an oven preheated to 180°C (350°F) for 30 minutes or until the tomatoes are tender.

Serves 2

Spinach Stuffing

The commercially packed seasoning mix used in this recipe is a tasty combination of pepper, salt, pimiento and allspice.

6 large tomatoes
80 g butter
½ cup finely chopped onion
500 g spinach, chopped,
    cooked and well drained
1 tablespoon seasoning mix
½ teaspoon dried thyme
½ cup fresh breadcrumbs
2 eggs, beaten
½ cup grated Parmesan
    cheese

Prepare the tomatoes and set aside. Heat the butter in a shallow pan and gently fry the onion until soft but not browned. Add the spinach, seasoning, thyme and breadcrumbs, mix in the eggs and cook, stirring constantly, until well combined.

Spoon the mixture into each shell, sprinkle with the grated cheese and dot with additional butter. Bake in an oven preheated to 180°C (350°F) for 15 minutes or until brown on top and heated through.

Serves 4–6

Continental Beans Baked in Tomatoes

4–6 medium-sized tomatoes
30 g butter
1 clove garlic, crushed
2 onions, chopped
440 g can three bean
*   mix, drained*
1½ tablespoons tomato paste
½ teaspoon dried basil
½ teaspoon sugar
1 cup tomato puree
2 cups cooked brown rice,
*   hot*
1 tablespoon chopped
*   parsley, to garnish*

Prepare the tomatoes, reserving the pulp, and set aside. Melt the butter in a large pan, add the garlic and onions and cook for 1 minute. Stir in the beans, tomato paste, basil, sugar, tomato puree and reserved tomato pulp. Bring to the boil, then simmer for 20 minutes or until the sauce has thickened.

Spoon the bean mix into the tomato shells, then spoon the rice into individual 2-cup souffle dishes. Add the filled tomatoes, topping with any additional bean mix. Bake in an oven preheated to 200°C (400°F) for 5–10 minutes. Serve sprinkled with chopped parsley.

Serves 4–6

Cashew and Brown Rice Tomatoes

6 medium-sized tomatoes
30 g butter
4 shallots (spring onions,
*   scallions), chopped*
1 cup brown rice, rinsed well
freshly ground black pepper
2 cups chicken stock
60 g cashew nuts
parsley, to garnish

Prepare the tomatoes, reserving the tops and pulp. Heat the butter in a large pan, add the shallots and rice and cook for 1 minute, stirring constantly. Add the pepper and chicken stock, cover the pan and bring the mixture to the boil. Reduce the heat and cook for 20 minutes or until all the liquid has evaporated.

When cooked, fold in the tomato pulp and cashews. Cook for another 10 minutes or until the pulp is well incorporated. Fill the tomato shells with the rice mixture and put into a baking dish. Place lids on top of tomatoes. Bake in an oven preheated to 190°C (375°F) for 10 minutes. Serve the tomatoes garnished with parsley.

Serves 6

Tomatoes with Avocado

The perfect accompaniment to poached fish.

6 medium-sized tomatoes,
*   cored and peeled*
salt and pepper, to taste
1 large ripe avocado,
*   chopped*
¼ cup Vinaigrette (see recipe)
1 green or red capsicum,
*   (pepper)*
1 tablespoon finely chopped
*   shallots*
1 tablespoon chopped dill
*   or 1 teaspoon dried dill*

Slice off the round end of the tomatoes and scoop out the seeds and membranes. Season shell with salt and pepper, invert and leave to drain.

Combine the avocado with the remaining ingredients, cover and chill for 30 minutes. Spoon the avocado mixture into the tomato shells.

Serves 6

Cottage Tomatoes

Choose firm tomatoes as these hold their shape during baking.

6 medium-sized tomatoes
2 cloves garlic, crushed
2 tablespoons chopped
*   shallots (spring onions,*
*   scallions)*
30 g butter
few mushroom stalks,
*   chopped (optional)*
2 tablespoons finely chopped
*   parsley*
salt and pepper, to taste
1 cup dry breadcrumbs
1 tablespoon grated
*   Parmesan cheese*
1–2 tablespoons olive oil

Halve the tomatoes and scoop out the seeds and membranes. Pat tomato shells dry with a paper towel.

Cook the garlic and shallots in butter until tender (about 3 minutes). Add the remaining ingredients (except for the olive oil) and stir well to combine. Spoon the mixture into each tomato case and sprinkle lightly with oil. Place on baking tray and bake in an oven preheated to 190°C (375°F) for 25 minutes.

Serves 6

Middle Eastern Tomatoes

8–10 large tomatoes
½ cup olive oil
2 onions, finely chopped
¾ cup rice
2 tablespoons currants
2 tablespoons pine nuts
2 tablespoons finely chopped
    mint
2 tablespoons finely chopped
    parsley
salt and pepper to taste
1¼ cups water

Prepare the tomatoes, reserving the pulp and tops. Heat the oil in a pan and saute the onions until browned. Stir in the tomato pulp, then mix in the remaining ingredients. Simmer for 2 minutes, then add 1¼ cups water and cook slowly for 7 minutes or until the rice begins to soften. Season to taste.

Spoon the mixture into the tomato shells, allowing room at the top for the rice to swell. Replace the tops and brush all over with oil. Arrange on an oiled baking tray and cook in an oven preheated to 180°C (350°F) for 35–40 minutes.

Serves 4–5

Turkish Tomatoes

8–10 large tomatoes
¼ cup oil
2 onions, finely chopped
2 medium-sized eggplants
    (aubergines), chopped
½ cup finely grated fresh
    breadcrumbs
3 tablespoons finely chopped
    parsley
salt and pepper, to taste
¾ cup finely grated cheese
2 eggs, beaten

Prepare the tomatoes, reserving the pulp. Heat the oil in a pan, add onions and cook until lightly browned. Add the tomato pulp and simmer for 5 minutes. Stir in the eggplant and simmer for 5 minutes, or until tender. Add the breadcrumbs, together with the parsley and seasoning. Cook, stirring for 2 minutes.

Remove the pan from the heat and beat in the cheese. Stir in the eggs and mix thoroughly. Spoon the mixture into each tomato shell and arrange in a greased ovenproof dish. Bake in an oven preheated to 180°C (350°F) for 30 minutes or until tender.

Serves 4–6

Chicken Livers in Tomato Shells

4–6 medium-sized tomatoes
500 g chicken livers,
    trimmed, washed and
    drained
1 tablespoon flour
salt and pepper to taste
½ teaspoon dried mustard
60 g butter
1 onion, sliced
125 g button mushrooms
3 bacon rashers, chopped,
    rind removed
1 tablespoon finely chopped
    parsley
¼ cup dry white wine
2 cups boiled rice, hot
watercress, to garnish

Prepare the tomatoes, reserving the tops and the pulp. Coat the chicken livers in the flour seasoned with salt, pepper and mustard.

Melt the butter in a frying pan and cook the livers gently for 5 minutes, then remove from pan and set aside. Add onion, mushroom, bacon and parsley to the pan and cook for 1–2 minutes.

Pour in the wine and increase the heat, scraping the base of the pan to loosen the sediment. Return the livers to the frying pan and simmer for 10 minutes. Fill the tomato shells with the chicken liver mixture.

Spoon a portion of rice onto individual plates, place a tomato on the rice and top with the lid. Garnish with watercress and serve.

Serves 4–6

Tomatoes with Tuna

6 medium-sized tomatoes,
    cored and peeled
200 g can tuna
    packed in oil
3 eggs, hard-boiled and
    chopped
1 tablespoon chopped shallot
    (spring onion, scallion)
squeeze lemon juice
salt and pepper, to taste
1 tablespoon chopped dill, to
    garnish

Cut off the top third of the tomatoes and scoop out the seeds and membrane.

Drain the tuna well and flake with a fork. Combine with the eggs, shallot and lemon juice. Season to taste with salt and pepper.

Spoon into the tomato cases and serve garnished with the dill.

Serves 6

Cherry Tomatoes Filled with Hummus

1 cup chick peas, soaked
  overnight
½ cup tahini
3 tablespoons lemon juice
salt, cayenne pepper and
  paprika, to taste
1 punnet cherry tomatoes
2 tablespoons chopped
  parsley
1½ tablespoons oil

Cook the chick peas in 1½ cups water to cover. Bring to the boil, reduce the heat and simmer for 1½ hours until tender. Drain and reserve the liquid. Reserve ½ cup chick peas for the garnish. Puree the peas with the garlic in a food processor or blender. Blend in the tahini and lemon juice, then add a little of the reserved cooking liquid to make a thick, creamy consistency. Season with the salt, cayenne pepper and paprika to taste. Chill the hummus, covered with plastic wrap, for 2 hours.

Prepare the cherry tomatoes, brush the rims of the drained shells with oil and dip into the chopped parsley to coat the rim. Pipe the hummus into each case and drizzle a few drops of oil over the top. Garnish with the reserved chick peas.

Note: This dish may be prepared ahead and stored, covered, in the refrigerator for 3 hours.

Makes about 30

Cherry Tomatoes with Egg Filling

1 punnet cherry tomatoes
6 hard-boiled eggs
⅓ cup mayonnaise
200 g ham, diced
1 tablespoon chopped
  parsley
squeeze lemon juice
salt and pepper, to taste

Prepare the cherry tomatoes, reserving the tops. Separate the egg yolks and press through a fine sieve. Add the mayonnaise to the yolks and mix until smooth. Chop the egg whites very finely and add them to the mayonnaise mixture with salt and pepper.

Fill the tomato shells with the egg mixture. Replace the tomato tops at an angle. Chill, covered, for 3 hours before serving.

Makes about 30

Eggplant with Vegetable Filling

2 medium-sized eggplants
  (aubergines)
oil, for frying
1 small onion, chopped
250 g mushrooms, chopped
1 tablespoon chopped
  parsley
125 g tomato, cored, peeled
  and chopped

salt and pepper, to taste
½ cup fine breadcrumbs
½ cup Parmesan or tasty
  cheese
20 g butter
Fresh Tomato Sauce (see
  recipe)

Cut the eggplant in half lengthways, then with the point of a small knife, make a cut around each half 5 mm from the edge to loosen the flesh. Care should be taken not to cut through the skin. Make several more cuts, 5 mm deep, across the centre of each eggplant. Deep fry the eggplant in hot oil for 3 minutes, then carefully scoop out the pulp and chop it finely. Leave the shell intact.

Heat a little oil in a saucepan and gently fry the onion until tender. Add the chopped mushrooms and cook gently for a few minutes more. Mix the eggplant pulp, parsley, tomato and salt and pepper. Spoon the mixture into the eggplant skins.

Combine the breadcrumbs with the cheese and butter and sprinkle it over the top. Brown under a grill or in a hot oven. Serve with the hot, fresh Tomato Sauce.

Serves 4

Baked Capsicums and Tomato

2 red capsicums (peppers),
  halved lengthways and
  seeded
2 green capsicums (peppers),
  halved lengthways and
  seeded
2 yellow capsicums (peppers)
  if available, or 1 extra red
  and green capsicum,
  halved and seeded

3 cloves garlic, thinly sliced
salt and pepper, to taste
2 large tomatoes, cored,
  peeled and seeded
30 g butter
1–2 tablespoons olive oil
2 tablespoons chopped
  parsley, to garnish

Place 2 or 3 slices of garlic into each capsicum half, then season with salt and pepper. Roughly chop the tomatoes and divide evenly between the capsicums. Dot with butter and sprinkle each capsicum with a little olive oil. Place the capsicums in a lightly greased baking dish and bake in an oven preheated to 180°C (350°F) for 25 minutes. Serve hot sprinkled with the parsley.

Serves 6–12

Note: If the flavour of the garlic is too strong for some tastes, peel one clove of garlic and rub it over the inside of the capsicums. The capsicums can also be wrapped in aluminium foil and heated over the barbecue, then served as an accompaniment to barbecued meat.

THE MAIN COURSE

By experimenting, you will discover the richer colour and added tang that tomatoes or tomato products such as tomato paste or puree bring to many main courses.
With meat, chicken and fish, tomatoes provide a nutritious addition. The same applies to vegetarian dishes such as Cauliflower and Tomato Gratin.

Veal Parmigiana

Spanish Pot Roast

1 kg piece round steak
salt and pepper, to taste
½ cup flour
4 tablespoons olive oil
2 large onions, chopped
1 cup tomato juice
180 g can tomato paste
3 large tomatoes, cored,
   peeled and chopped
½ teaspoon chilli powder
1 clove garlic, chopped
2 bay leaves
½ teaspoon sugar
¼ teaspoon basil
6 olives, sliced, and chopped
   parsley, to garnish

Pound the steak to flatten, then season it with salt and pepper. Sprinkle with the flour on both sides.

Heat the oil in a large pan and cook the onions until brown. Add the steak and brown it on both sides. Pour in the tomato juice, paste, chopped tomatoes, chilli, garlic, bay leaves, sugar and basil. Simmer, covered for 1–1½ hours or until tender, adding extra tomato juice if necessary.

Remove the steak and cut it into thick slices. Spoon some sauce onto a heated platter and arrange the sliced steak on top. Coat with extra sauce, then garnish with the olives and parsley.

Serves 6

Chilli con Carne

Like curries, Chilli con Carne improves in flavour if made in advance. It freezes well and is suitable for a main course or informal meal.

1 tablespoon oil
1 medium-sized onion, sliced
500 g minced topside
1 medium-sized green
   capsicum (pepper),
   chopped
1 clove garlic, finely chopped
425 g can tomato pieces
465 g can red kidney
   beans, drained
250 g can tomato paste
1½–2 teaspoons chilli
   powder
1 teaspoon salt
1 tablespoon chopped fresh
   basil

Heat the oil in a large pan, add the onion, crumble in the mince and fry over high heat for 5 minutes. Pour off any excess fat, then stir in the remaining ingredients. Bring the mixture to the boil, cover and simmer for 1 hour, stirring occasionally. Serve with rice.

Serves 6

Curried Meat Balls

750 g minced beef
2 eggs, beaten
2 slices bread, soaked in milk
   then squeezed dry
1 small onion, finely chopped
freshly ground black pepper
1 tablespoon curry powder
4 medium-sized potatoes,
   diced
2 carrots, diced
1¼ cups tomato puree
pinch cayenne pepper
pinch cumin
pinch coriander

Mix the beef, eggs, bread, onion and pepper with 2 teaspoons of curry powder. Shape the mixture into walnut-sized balls, and set aside.

Cook the potatoes and carrots in sufficient water to cover for 10 minutes. Add the meat balls, remaining curry powder, tomato puree, cayenne pepper, cumin and coriander and simmer for 30 minutes. Serve over boiled rice.

Serves 6

Braised Beef Capsicums

¼ cup long grain rice
250 g minced beef
salt and pepper, to taste
pinch oregano
4 medium-sized green
   capsicums (peppers)
425 g canned tomato
   soup

Cook the rice in boiling salted water until tender, approximately 12 minutes. Drain. Mix the rice with the beef and seasoning. Cut the stem end off each capsicum and remove the seeds and membrane. Spoon the filling into the capsicums, and replace lids.

Place the capsicums in a small saucepan so that they fit snugly and stand upright. Pour over the tomato soup. Cover and simmer gently for 1 hour or until the capsicums are soft. Serve with some tomato soup spooned over.

Serves 4

1 Cut the stem end from each capsicum and remove the seeds and membrane

2 Spoon the filling into the capsicums

3 Stand the capsicums upright in a small saucepan and pour over the tomato soup

Braised Beef Capsicums

Easy Lasagne

Most lasagne recipes are long and involved; layer upon layer of sauce, pasta and meat. Here is a recipe that is simple but not lacking flavour.

500 g cooked lasagne
250 g cream cheese, softened
250 g cottage cheese
300 mL sour (dairy soured) cream
2 tablespoons oil
1 green capsicum (pepper), seeded and chopped
1 large onion, chopped

500 g minced beef
salt and pepper, to taste
850 g can tomatoes, drained and chopped
300 g mushrooms, chopped
½ teaspoon basil
½ teaspoon sugar
1½ cups grated cheese

Drain the lasagne and rinse in warm water. Arrange a layer in a greased ovenproof dish approximately 17 x 25 cm. Mix the cream cheese, cottage cheese and sour cream, and spread over the lasagne.

Heat the oil in a frying pan and cook onion and green capsicum until soft. Stir in the beef, salt and pepper and brown lightly. Drain off excess fat. Add the tomatoes and mushrooms, basil and sugar. Cook for 20 minutes or until thickened and well combined.

Spoon over the sauce and top with more lasagne and the grated cheese. Bake in oven preheated to 180°C (350°F) for 1 hour or until golden and bubbling. Serve with green salad.

Serves 6–8

Savoury Mince

An excellent way of using up very ripe or cooking tomatoes.

2 tablespoons oil
2 onions, sliced
2 cloves garlic, crushed
500 g minced steak
1.5 kg tomatoes, cored, peeled and chopped
2 carrots, sliced
1 tablespoon Worcestershire sauce
1 tablespoon chopped fresh basil or 1 teaspoon dried basil
¼ teaspoon cayenne pepper
salt and pepper, to taste

Heat the oil in a pan and gently fry the onions and garlic until soft but not browned. Add the mince and cook, stirring, until crumbly and browned. Mix in the remaining ingredients and simmer, uncovered, for 30–45 minutes, stirring occasionally.

Serve on toast or in bowls with crusty bread.
Note: This dish is also delicious reheated.

Serves 6

Veal with Artichokes

¼ cup oil
1 clove garlic
1 kg veal, cut into 2.5 cm cubes
¼ cup flour, seasoned with salt and pepper
500 g canned tomato pieces
½ cup sauterne or sherry
¼ teaspoon oregano
salt and pepper, to taste
400 g can artichoke hearts, drained

Heat the oil in a pan and gently fry the garlic. Toss the veal in the seasoned flour, and then brown in the oil. Add the tomatoes, wine, oregano and seasoning. Mix well.

Cover the pan and simmer for 1 hour or until the veal is tender. Cut the artichokes into halves, add to the sauce and cook until heated through. Serve over hot pasta.

Serves 4

Veal Parmigiana

Pounding the veal scallops before cooking will make them tender. Place veal between two sheets of plastic wrap and pound with a rolling pin or meat mallet.

1 cup dried breadcrumbs
¾ cup grated Parmesan cheese
12 thin slices veal scallops
2 eggs, beaten
4 tablespoons oil
1 large onion, chopped
1 clove garlic, chopped

1 kg can tomato pieces, drained
¼ cup tomato paste
1 teaspoon basil
½ teaspoon thyme
salt and pepper, to taste
30–45 g butter
250 g mozzarella slices

Mix the breadcrumbs with ¼ cup of Parmesan cheese on a shallow plate. Dip the veal into the beaten egg, then coat with the crumb and cheese mixture. Stand until dry.

Heat half the oil in a pan and gently fry the onion and garlic until soft but not brown. Add the tomatoes, tomato paste, basil, thyme, salt and pepper, cover the pan and simmer for 15 minutes.

Heat the remaining oil and butter in a pan and brown the veal scallops on both sides, a few at a time. Add extra oil or butter if required.

Spoon part of the sauce into a shallow baking dish and arrange alternate, overlapping slices of veal and cheese in the dish. Spoon over the remaining sauce, sprinkle with the remaining Parmesan cheese and bake in an oven preheated to 170°C (340°F) for 20 minutes. Serve with a mixed green salad.

Serves 6

Mediterranean Veal Cutlets

3 kg veal cutlets
flour seasoned with salt and
    pepper
1½ tablespoons olive oil
20 g butter
1 large onion, chopped
8 ripe tomatoes, cored,
    peeled and quartered
1 cup white wine
2 bay leaves
½ teaspoon thyme
1 teaspoon chopped parsley
250 g button mushrooms,
    sliced
½ cup black olives

Dust the cutlets in the seasoned flour. Heat the olive oil and butter in a pan and brown the cutlets on both sides. Add the remaining ingredients, except the mushrooms and olives. Simmer gently for 1½–2 hours or until the veal is tender. Add the mushrooms and olives, simmer for 10 minutes longer, then serve.

Serves 8

Veal Marengo

The Marengo was a dish created by Napoleon's French chef to mark the victory of the battle of Marengo in 1800. The original recipe contained ingredients found close by the battlefield, including chicken and freshwater crayfish.

2 tablespoons oil
1 kg veal, cut into 2.5 cm
    cubes
2 medium-sized onions,
    finely chopped
1 tablespoon flour
2 tablespoons tomato paste
½ cup white wine
1 cup beef stock
2 cloves garlic, finely
    chopped
1 bouquet garni
250 g tomatoes, cored,
    peeled and chopped
freshly ground black pepper
1 teaspoon sage
1 teaspoon sugar
365 g can champignons,
    drained
8 fried heart-shaped bread
    croutes and finely chopped
    parsley, for garnish

Heat the oil in a pan and gently fry the veal in small batches for 3–4 minutes. Remove from the pan, add extra oil if necessary, then fry the onions until golden. Stir in the flour and cook until brown. Blend in the tomato paste, white wine and stock and heat, stirring until boiling.

Add the veal, garlic, bouquet garni and tomatoes, then season to taste with salt and pepper, sage and sugar. Cover the pan and simmer gently for 40 minutes. Add the champignons and continue cooking for 10–12 minutes until the meat is tender. Serve garnished with the croutes and parsley.

Serves 4–6

Barbecued Pork Spare Ribs

2 tablespoons oil
2 cloves garlic, chopped
125 g onions, finely chopped
¾ cup tomato puree
½ cup vinegar
½ cup honey
pinch basil
1 teaspoon mustard powder
2 tablespoons Worcestershire
    sauce
1 cup brown stock
2 kg pork spare ribs

Heat the oil in a pan and gently fry the garlic and onion until softened. Mix in the tomato puree, vinegar, honey, basil, mustard powder, Worcestershire sauce and stock. Bring to the boil, then reduce the heat and simmer for 15 minutes. Remove from the heat.

Put the ribs into the cooked barbecue marinade and marinate for 30 minutes.

Place a cake cooler over a roasting dish and arrange the ribs, fat-side up, on the cooler. Brush the ribs liberally with the sauce. Roast in an oven preheated to 200–230°C (400–440°F) for approximately 1 hour, basting the ribs every 15 minutes, or barbecue over medium heat, turning frequently. When cooked, cut the ribs into individual portions to serve. Serve with a crisp salad or fried rice.

Serves 4

Barbecued Pork Spare Ribs

Pork Chop Risotto

1 tablespoon oil
6 thick pork chops, trimmed
    of excess fat
⅔ cup rice
½ teaspoon turmeric
1 cup stock or water
freshly ground black pepper
1 large onion, chopped
425 g can tomatoes,
    drained and chopped
1 cup whole corn kernels

Heat the oil in a large pan, brown the chops, then remove and drain off excess fat. Spread the rice over the bottom of the pan. Stir the turmeric into the stock and season with pepper. Pour the stock over rice.

Arrange the chops on top of the rice, add the onion and tomatoes and spoon over the corn kernels. Bring to the boil over moderate heat, reduce the heat, cover and simmer for 25 minutes, adding more stock if necessary.

Serves 6
Note: This dish may also be baked in an oven preheated to 150°C (300°F) for 2 hours.

Pork Chop Risotto

Mild Lamb and Yoghurt Curry

Not everyone enjoys hot curry, so if in doubt, serve this Mild Lamb and Yoghurt Curry to your guests when entertaining.

750 g lean lamb
½ cup natural yoghurt
½ teaspoon salt
25 g ghee or butter
3 medium-sized onions,
    chopped
2 tablespoons garam masala
¼ teaspoon chilli powder
3 cloves garlic, crushed
375 g tomatoes, cored,
    peeled and chopped
60 g coconut cream

Cut the lamb into 2.5 cm cubes. Mix the yoghurt and salt together in a non-metallic dish and add the lamb. Marinate for 30 minutes, then drain.

Heat the ghee in a pan and fry onions then add the garam masala and chilli powder. Cook for 2 minutes, stirring. Add the garlic, lamb and tomatoes and bring to the boil. Blend in the coconut cream, cover the pan and cook over low heat for 1½ hours or until the lamb is tender.

Serves 4–6

Lamb Chops Italian Style

12 short loin lamb chops,
    boned and skinned

Sauce
3 tablespoons grated
    Parmesan cheese
3 tablespoons finely chopped
    parsley
salt and pepper, to taste
2 cloves garlic, finely
    chopped
1 cup Fresh Tomato Sauce
    (see recipe)
1 tablespoon chopped fresh
    basil
watercress springs, to garnish

Roll the thin end of each chop around the meaty section, and fasten with a toothpick. Combine all the sauce ingredients.

Season the chops with salt and pepper, then brush with the oil. Place on a greased baking tray and grill quickly for 2–3 minutes each side under a hot grill to seal the meat. Baste with sauce and continue cooking on a lower heat for 12–15 minutes. Turn and baste the chops several times during cooking. Serve garnished with watercress.

Serves 4–6

Lamb Koftas in Tomato Sauce

750 g lean lamb, minced
1 large onion, grated
2 teaspoons finely chopped
   parsley
3 slices wholemeal bread,
   soaked in water and
   squeezed dry
2 eggs
freshly ground black pepper,
   to taste
2 tablespoons flour, seasoned
   with salt and pepper
30 g ghee or butter
3 medium-sized ripe
   tomatoes, chopped
1 cup stock

Mix the lamb, onion, parsley, bread, eggs, salt and pepper together in a bowl. Shape the mixture into walnut-size balls, then roll in the seasoned flour.

Heat the ghee in a pan and brown the lamb koftas. Add the tomatoes and stock, cover the pan and simmer 30 minutes.

Serve with rice and mint sauce.

Serves 4–6

1 Brown chicken pieces in a frying pan, cooking until golden

2 Cook the onions and mushrooms in the same pan

3 Add the brown sauce and chopped tomatoes

Chicken and Mushrooms

1.5 kg chicken
60 g butter
2 tablespoons oil
salt and pepper, to taste
1 small onion, chopped
125 g button mushrooms,
   sliced
3 tablespoons white wine
1¼ cups Brown Sauce (see
   recipe)
250 g tomatoes, cored,
   peeled and chopped
chopped parsley, to garnish

Cut the legs off the chicken and cut in two at the joint. Remove the wish bone and wing tips, leaving two equal portions on the breast. Slice off the breast and cut in two. Reserve the carcass for stock.

Heat the butter and oil in a large pan. Season the chicken and add it to the pan in the following order: drumsticks, thighs, wings and breast. Cook until golden. Cover the pan with a lid and cook for approximately 20 minutes or until tender, then transfer to a serving dish and keep warm.

Add the onion to the pan and fry for 2 minutes, stir in the mushrooms, cover the pan and cook gently for 4 minutes. Drain off the fat, add the white wine and boil until reduced by half. Mix in the brown sauce and chopped tomatoes, and simmer for 5 minutes. Taste and adjust the seasoning if necessary. Pour the sauce over the chicken, then sprinkle with the parsley.

Serves 4

Lamb Koftas in Tomato Sauce

Chicken Cacciatore

Very ripe tomatoes, usually sold for less than salad tomatoes, make this an economical special occasion dish.

1.5 kg chicken pieces	2 teaspoons sugar
4 tablespoons flour, seasoned with salt and pepper	500 g cooking tomatoes
2 tablespoons oil	¼ cup tomato paste
1 onion, cut into 1 cm dice	½ teaspoon basil or oregano
1 clove garlic, chopped	½ cup dry white wine
½ red capsicum (pepper), seeded, cut into 1 cm dice	10 black olives
	Italian parsley, chopped, to garnish

Coat the chicken pieces with the seasoned flour, shaking off any excess flour.

Heat the oil in a frying pan and fry the chicken pieces for a few minutes on each side. Remove from the pan. Add a little extra oil if necessary, then gently fry the onion, garlic and capsicum for 3 minutes. Blend in the remaining ingredients and return the chicken pieces to the pan. Cover, bring to the boil, reduce the heat and simmer for 45 minutes or until the chicken is tender.

Adjust seasonings if necessary, and thicken the sauce with a little cornflour that has been blended with cold water. Sprinkle over the parsley, and serve with pasta.

Serves 4

Chicken Cacciatore

Stir-fried Chicken with Tomatoes and Black Beans

Tomatoes are seldom found in recipes from the Orient but their flavour blends beautifully with eastern herbs and spices.

1 tablespoon black beans	pepper, to taste
2 whole chicken breast fillets	2 teaspoons soy sauce
4 tomatoes, cored and peeled	1 tablespoon cornflour
2 small cloves garlic	1 cup chicken stock
2 tablespoons dry sherry	3 tablespoons oil
2 teaspoons sugar	

Soak the black beans in warm water to cover for 5 minutes, then drain. Cut chicken in 2.5 cm cubes. Cut the tomatoes to a similar size. Roughly chop the black beans and garlic. Combine the sherry, sugar, pepper and soy sauce in a small bowl. In another bowl, blend the cornflour, and half the stock to make a smooth paste.

Heat oil in a large pan and fry the black beans and garlic for 1–3 minutes. Add the cubed chicken, stir for 4 minutes or until the flesh turns white. Sprinkle over the sherry mixture and fry for 2 minutes more. Pour in the remaining stock and cook on high, then reduce the heat to medium and cook, covered, for a further 6 minutes. Stir in the tomatoes and cook until heated through. Blend in the cornflour mixture and stir until thickened. Serve hot with rice.

Serves 4–6

Stir-fried Chicken with Tomatoes and Black Beans

Prawn and Scallop Sate with Tomato Rice

Before using plunge the bamboo skewers into a pan of boiling water, then drain. This prevents them burning.

18 green king prawns,
*   shelled and deveined*
24 scallops
2 tablespoons olive oil
¼ cup coconut cream
1 clove garlic, crushed
½ teaspoon cumin
2 teaspoons turmeric
1 tablespoon sugar
1 tablespoon water
salt and pepper, to taste
2 tablespoons sesame seeds
6 lemon twists and cherry
*   tomatoes, to garnish*

Tomato Rice
20 g butter
1 onion, finely chopped
2 tomatoes, peeled and
*   chopped*
⅓ cup tomato juice
2½ cups chicken stock
1½ tablespoons tomato paste
200 g long grain rice, rinsed
1½ tablespoons oil
3 tablespoons wine vinegar
freshly ground black pepper

Thread prawns and scallops alternately onto 6 bamboo skewers. Arrange in a single layer in a shallow dish. Combine olive oil, coconut cream, garlic, cumin, turmeric, sugar, water and salt and pepper. Pour the marinade over the seafood and marinate in the refrigerator for 1 hour.

Meanwhile prepare the rice. Melt the butter in a large saucepan and cook the onion gently until transparent. Add the tomatoes and tomato juice and bring to the boil. Add the chicken stock and return to the boil. Mix the tomato paste, rice, oil, wine vinegar and pepper and continue to boil until the excess liquid has evaporated. Reduce the heat, cover the pan and simmer for 7 minutes or until the rice is tender to the bite.

Cook the sate under a preheated grill for 2 minutes each side. Spoon a portion of rice onto individual serving plates. Place the sate sticks on the rice, then sprinkle with sesame seeds. Garnish with lemon twists and cherry tomatoes.

Serves 6

Seafood in Wine Sauce

Seafood in Wine Sauce

300 g uncooked prawns,
*   shelled and deveined*
125 g seafood sticks
125 g thick fish fillet
125 g scallops
flour, seasoned with salt and
*   pepper*
2 tablespoons oil
1 clove garlic, chopped

250 g ripe tomatoes, cored,
*   peeled and chopped*
⅔ cup Fresh Tomato Sauce
*   (see recipe)*
1½ tablespoons white wine
salt and pepper, to taste
2 tablespoons chopped
*   parsley*

Cut the prawns, seafood sticks and fish fillets into 2.5 cm lengths. Coat all the seafood in the seasoned flour, shaking off any excess. Heat the oil in a frying pan until hot, then add the seafood. Fry until light golden colour, turning frequently, then drain the seafood on absorbent paper.

Add the garlic to the pan and fry gently for 1 minute. Stir in the tomatoes and sauce and cook for 10 minutes more. Remove from the pan, add the wine and simmer until reduced by half, then return the tomatoes to the pan together with tomato sauce and bring to a boil. Season to taste with salt and pepper. Add the parsley and mix in the seafood. Serve with rice.

Serves 4

Prawn and Scallop Sate, Mussel Boats (see recipe)

Baked Fish Creole Style

Serve with crusty bread so that the sauce may be enjoyed to the fullest.

Creole Sauce

20 g butter
1 tablespoon flour
1 cup tomato juice, fresh or
    canned
½ cup white wine
1 small onion, finely chopped
1 tablespoon finely chopped
    parsley
1 small carrot, grated
1 clove garlic, crushed

½ red capsicum (pepper),
    seeded and finely chopped
½ green capsicum (pepper),
    seeded and finely chopped
pinch cayenne pepper
½ teaspoon salt
juice of 1 lemon, strained
1 stalk celery, finely chopped
250 g mushrooms, finely
    chopped

Fish and Filling

1 medium-sized snapper or
    large bream, cleaned and
    scaled
1 onion, finely chopped
15 g butter

1 green capsicum (pepper),
    seeded and finely chopped
400 g can crabmeat,
    drained and flaked

1 Trim fish tail and fins using kitchen scissors

2 Spoon crab mixture into the cavity of the fish

3 Pour the remaining Creole sauce over the fish

Heat 20 g butter in a pan, add the flour, stirring until smooth. Cook over a medium heat until brown. Gradually add tomato juice and wine, stirring until smooth, then add the remaining ingredients. Simmer for 30 minutes. Cover and keep warm over very low heat while preparing the fish.

Melt 15 g butter in a pan, cook the onion until softened, approximately 5 minutes. Add the capsicum and crabmeat, mixing well. Set aside until cool.

Trim the fish tail and fins using kitchen scissors. Season the cavity of the fish and spoon in the crab mixture. Secure the opening with skewers or toothpicks. Pour half the sauce in a greased baking dish large enough to hold the fish. Place the fish onto the sauce and pour over the remaining sauce. Bake in an oven preheated to 175°C (350°F) for 30–45 minutes or until the flesh flakes easily. Baste frequently with the sauce during baking.

Serves 6

Baked Fish Fillet Gratin

30 g butter
2 tablespoons savoury biscuit
    crumbs
500 g thick fish fillets, ling or
    gem fish

1 cup canned tomato pieces
1 medium-sized onion, finely
    chopped
salt and pepper, to taste
½ cup grated cheese

Grease a shallow baking dish with half the butter and sprinkle over the biscuit crumbs. Place the fillets on the crumbs.

Combine the tomatoes, onion, salt and pepper and pour the mixture over the fish. Dot with the remaining butter and the cheese. Bake in an oven preheated to 175°C (350°F) for 35 minutes or until the fish flakes easily.

Serves 2

Seafood Curry

2 tablespoons lemon juice
250 g fish fillets, cut into bite-
    size pieces
250 g uncooked prawns,
    peeled and deveined
125 g scallops
60 g calamari rings
60 g mussels in shell, cleaned
2 tablespoons olive oil
2 onions, chopped
1 teaspoon grated ginger
2 cloves garlic
½ teaspoon chilli powder

½ teaspoon cumin
¼ teaspoon garam masala
¼ teaspoon coriander
1 teaspoon turmeric
2 medium tomatoes, peeled
    and chopped
grated rind ½ lemon
½ cup water
2 cups boiled rice, hot
½ tablespoon chopped
    parsley
6 lemon twists, to garnish

Combine the lemon juice, fish, prawns, scallops and calamari in a dish and set aside to marinate.

Heat the olive oil in a large pan. Add mussels and cook over high heat for 5–7 minutes until the shells open. Transfer the mussels to a separate dish discarding any shells that have not opened. Set aside.

Add the remaining ingredients, except the cooked rice and parsley, to the olive oil. Bring to the boil, lower heat and simmer for 20 minutes. Add the seafood marinade to the pan and simmer for 10 minutes longer.

Spoon the rice into a circle onto 6 individual plates, then spoon the seafood curry into the centre. Place the mussels onto the side of the plates. Sprinkle over the chopped parsley and garnish with lemon twists, then serve.

Serves 6

Layered Vegetable Mornay

1 tablespoon vegetable oil
1 medium-sized onion, finely
  chopped
250 g button mushrooms,
  sliced
½ red capsicum (pepper), cut
  1 cm dice
½ green capsicum (pepper),
  cut 1 cm dice
2 tablespoons fresh basil
  chopped, or 2 teaspoons
  dried basil leaves

Spinach Layer

1 bunch English spinach or
  silver beet, washed, stalks
  removed and chopped
1 clove garlic, finely chopped
1 medium-sized onion, finely
  chopped
¼ teaspoon nutmeg

Mornay Sauce

¾ cup milk
¼ cup onion, roughly
  chopped
4 whole cloves
1 bay leaf
30 g butter
2 tablespoons flour
½ cup grated cheese

440 g can tomato pieces,
  drained and chopped
4 tablespoons tomato paste
1 teaspoon sugar
6–8 zucchinis (courgettes),
  ends trimmed and sliced
  into 5 mm lengths
extra grated Parmesan
  cheese

Cheese Layer

500 g ricotta cheese
½ cup grated Parmesan
  cheese
2 x 60 g eggs, beaten.

Heat the oil in a large pan and gently fry the onion, mushrooms and capsicums until tender. Add the basil, tomatoes, tomato paste and sugar. Simmer, uncovered, for 30 minutes, then set aside.

Meanwhile, to prepare the spinach layer, place the spinach leaves, garlic, onion and nutmeg into a saucepan and cook, covered, for 3–5 minutes or until the spinach has wilted. Drain well, squeezing the spinach to remove all excess liquid. Set aside.

To make the Mornay Sauce, heat the milk with the onion, cloves and bay leaf. Strain, discard flavourings and cool. Melt the butter in a heavy based saucepan and add the flour. Cook for 1 minute or until foaming but not brown. Whisk in the milk and cook, stirring until boiling. Fold in the cheese and remove from the heat and cover closely with waxed paper until required.

Combine the ricotta and Parmesan cheeses with the eggs and reserve.

To assemble, pour half the vegetable mixture into a greased casserole dish and top with a layer of zucchini strips. Top with the spinach mixture, remaining vegetable mixture, ricotta and Parmesan cheese. Cover with the remaining zucchini strips. Pour the Mornay Sauce evenly over and sprinkle with the extra cheese. Bake in an oven preheated to 190°C (375°F) for 30–45 minutes or until the top is golden and bubbling.

Serves 4–6

Layered Vegetable Mornay

1 Pour boiling water over the whole cabbage to blanch and loosen the leaves

2 Carefully peel back the softened leaves occasionally pouring more water over the remaining cabbage

3 Using a sharp knife, cut the leaves away from the central core at the base

Cottage Vegetable Rolls

The outer leaves from the cabbage are the easiest to roll. Run hot water over the cabbage and the leaves will peel away.

8 flat cabbage leaves, stem
   section removed
1 tablespoon of oil
2 medium onions, finely
   chopped
1 green capsicum (pepper),
   finely chopped
1 tablespoon of tomato paste
1 cup cottage cheese
500 g tomatoes cored, peeled
   and chopped

2 cups cooked lentils
salt and pepper, to taste
½ teaspoon sugar
¼ teaspoon basil
¼ teaspoon oregano
3 tablespoons sesame seeds,
   toasted
sour (dairy soured) cream, for
   serving

Steam the cabbage leaves until tender. Heat the oil in a pan and gently fry the onions and capsicum until tender, then cool. Mix in the tomato paste, cottage cheese, tomatoes, lentils and seasonings and cook for 10 minutes more.

Divide the filling between the cabbage leaves and roll them up firmly. Arrange the rolls, seam side down, in a greased casserole dish in an oven preheated to 175°C (340°F) for 45 minutes. Sprinkle with sesame seeds and serve them with sour cream.

Serves 4–6

Tomato and Anchovy Cheese Bake

8 slices bread, crusts
   removed
60 g butter
750 g tomatoes, cored,
   peeled and thinly sliced
1 cup grated mozzarella
   cheese

50 g jar anchovy paste
1 cup grated Parmesan
   cheese
freshly ground black pepper
½ cup finely chopped pickled
   cucumbers
300 mL cream

Cut each slice of bread in half. Heat the butter in a frying pan and fry the bread until crisp and golden. Drain on absorbent paper, then arrange half the bread in the bottom of a greased, shallow ovenproof dish. Cover with a layer of tomatoes. Sprinkle over the mozzarella cheese, then spread the remaining pieces of bread thickly with anchovy paste. Arrange this layer of bread and then tomato, finishing with a layer of Parmesan cheese. Season with the pepper. Mix the cucumbers with the cream and pour over the dish. Bake in an oven preheated to 180°C (350°F) for 30 minutes.

Serves 6

Cauliflower and Tomato Gratin

1 cauliflower, cut into florets
500 g tomatoes, cored and
   peeled and roughly
   chopped
salt and pepper, to taste
100 g butter, melted

½ cup fresh breadcrumbs
½ cup grated Cheddar
   cheese
½ cup grated Parmesan
   cheese

Cook the cauliflower in boiling salted water until tender, then drain and refresh under cold running water.

Place the cauliflower and tomatoes in a greased dish and season with salt and pepper. Pour over half the butter. Combine the breadcrumbs and cheeses, sprinkle over and coat with the remaining butter.

Bake in an oven preheated to 190°C (375°F) for 30 minutes or until bubbling.

Serves 6

Egg and Tomato Crumble

75 g butter
4 onions, finely sliced
16 hard-boiled eggs, sliced
750 g tomatoes, cored,
   peeled and sliced
salt and pepper, to taste
1 cup grated tasty cheese
¼ cup fresh breadcrumbs

Melt the butter, reserving 15 g, and gently fry the onions for 10 minutes until soft but not browned. Spoon a layer of onion into the bottom of a greased, shallow ovenproof dish. Cover with a layer of eggs, then a layer of tomatoes and season to taste with salt and pepper. Continue making layers, finishing with a layer of tomatoes.

Mix the cheese and breadcrumbs together and sprinkle over the top, then dot with the remaining butter. Bake in an oven preheated to 200°C (400°F) for 30 minutes or until well browned.

Serves 8

Cauliflower and Tomato Gratin

Eggplant and Tomato Casserole

750 g eggplant (aubergine),
  peeled and sliced
2 eggs, beaten
30 g butter, melted
½ onion, finely chopped
½ teaspoon dried oregano
¼ cup dried breadcrumbs
salt and pepper, to taste
2 large tomatoes, thinly sliced
½ cup grated tasty cheese
¼ cup grated Parmesan
  cheese
paprika

Place the eggplant into a saucepan and cover with boiling water. Add a pinch of salt and cook over high heat for 10 minutes. Alternatively, cook the eggplant in a microwave oven, adding only a little water. Cook on high for 7 minutes. Stir after 5 minutes, adding the onion at the same time. Remove with a slotted spoon then chop and mash or process roughly in a food processor or blender. Mix the eggplant with the eggs, butter, onion, oregano, breadcrumbs, salt and pepper.

Arrange half the tomato slices in the bottom of a greased, shallow ovenproof dish. Spoon over the eggplant mixture and top with the remaining tomatoes. Mix the cheeses together and sprinkle over the tomatoes, then sprinkle lightly with the paprika.

Bake in an oven preheated to 190°C (375°F) for 45 minutes or until the cheese has browned.
Note: This dish can also be cooked in a microwave oven on medium for 8 minutes.

Serves 6

Golden-topped Vegetable Casserole

1 eggplant
2 carrots, peeled and sliced
2 potatoes, peeled and sliced
2 onions
¼ cup olive oil
4 zucchini
4 tomatoes
2 cups okra, canned or fresh
¼ cup chopped parsley
2 teaspoons oregano
salt and pepper
¼ teaspoon nutmeg
3 cups mashed potato
½ cup grated cheese
2 eggs
½ cup milk

Slice eggplant, sprinkle with salt and allow to stand 30 minutes.

Plunge the carrots and potatoes into boiling water and simmer for 5 minutes. Drain and rinse under cold water. Peel and slice onions. Rinse eggplant and pat dry. Fry onions in heated oil until soft. Remove and fry eggplant until golden brown. Slice zucchini and tomatoes. Top and tail okra.

In a deep casserole, layer all vegetables, sprinkling each layer with a little parsley, oregano, salt, pepper and nutmeg. Cover casserole and bake at 200°C (400°F) for 30 minutes.

Combine mashed potato, cheese, egg yolks, milk and paprika until smooth and creamy. Beat egg whites until stiff and fold into potato mixture. Spoon over casserole and place in oven. Bake at 190°C (375°F) until top is golden.

Serves 4–6

Herbed Bacon and Tomato Casserole

2 rashers bacon, rind
  removed
1 large onion
1 tablespoon chopped
  parsley
3 slices bread, crusts
  removed
½ teaspoon dried basil or 2
  teaspoons fresh basil
500 g tomatoes, cored,
  peeled and sliced
salt and pepper, to taste
25 g butter

Mince the bacon, onion, parsley, bread and basil in a food processor or blender.

Spoon the mixture into the bottom of a greased shallow ovenproof dish to form a thin layer. Cover with a layer of tomatoes and season with salt and pepper.

Continue making layers of mince and tomatoes, finishing with the minced mixture. Dot with the butter and bake in an oven preheated to 200°C (400°F) for 30 minutes or until well browned.

Serves 4

Individual Moussakas

4 small eggplants
1 tablespoon butter
1 tablespoon flour
½ teaspoon nutmeg
salt and pepper
¾ cup milk
¼ cup cream
2 onions
2 cloves garlic
1 tablespoon oil
2 tomatoes
2 cups cooked soy beans
1 tablespoon chopped
  parsley
¼ teaspoon oregano
1 cup grated Cheddar cheese
½ cup soft breadcrumbs

Slice eggplant in half lengthways, scoop out seeds, leaving flesh. Sprinkle with salt, turn upside down and allow to stand 30 minutes.

Melt butter in saucepan, stir in flour, nutmeg, salt and pepper; cook one minute. Gradually add milk, stirring until sauce thickens and boils. Cool slightly, stir in cream, cover and set aside.

Peel and chop onions and garlic, cook in oil 5 minutes. Add peeled, chopped tomatoes, soy beans, parsley and oregano. Simmer 15 minutes.

Rinse eggplant, pat dry, place in baking dish. Spoon equal quantities of mixture into each half. Cover with white sauce. Combine grated cheese and breadcrumbs, and sprinkle on top. Bake at 180°C (350°F) until eggplant is soft but not split. Place under griller to brown top before serving,

Serves 4

AFTERNOON TEA
A Meal in Itself

For those times when a piece of cake and a hot cup of tea is just what's needed, we offer these two delicious cakes which use tomato as a basic ingredient! Try them, you'll be delighted at their moist, fluffy texture. And your guests won't be able to guess what the mystery ingredient is.

Spicy Tomato Cake

The spicy aroma of this cake — fresh from the oven, draws everyone towards the kitchen!

125 g butter
2 cups brown sugar
2 teaspoons vanilla
4 cups flour, sifted
1 teaspoon bicarbonate of
   soda
2 teaspoons cinnamon
1 teaspoon nutmeg
½ teaspoon ground cloves
½ teaspoon mixed spice
2½ cups tomato puree
¾ cup chopped pecans

Icing

60 g cream cheese
30 g butter
1 cup icing sugar
1 teaspoon cinnamon
nutmeg, for garnish

Beat butter with sugar and vanilla until light and creamy. Fold in sifted flour, bicarbonate of soda and spices. Stir in tomato puree and pecans.

Pour batter into a greased 23 cm ring tin (gugelhopf or bundt) and bake in a preheated oven 180°C (350°F) for 60–70 minutes, or until a skewer inserted in the centre comes out clean. Cool in tin for 10 minutes, then turn onto a wire rack. Ice when cold. Beat cream cheese and butter until smooth. Gradually beat in icing sugar and cinnamon. Top cake with icing and sprinkle with nutmeg.

Tomato Devil's Food Cake

125 g cooking chocolate
1 cup soft brown sugar
¼ cup milk
3 eggs, separated
½ cup cornflour
1½ cups flour
1 teaspoon bicarbonate of
   soda
1 teaspoon cinnamon
125 g butter
¾ cup caster sugar
1 teaspoon vanilla
1¼ cups tomato puree

Icing

90 g cream cheese
60 g butter
1½ cups icing sugar
2 tablespoons cocoa powder
1 tablespoon brandy
   (optional)
shredded coconut, for
   garnish

Place chocolate, brown sugar, milk and 1 egg yolk in top of a double boiler over simmering water. Cook, stirring constantly, till smooth and slightly thickened then set aside to cool.

Sift flours, bicarbonate of soda and cinnamon. Cream butter, sugar and vanilla until light and fluffy. Beat in egg yolks one at a time, then stir in tomato puree, vanilla and the chocolate mixture. Fold in the sifted dry ingredients. Beat egg whites till stiff and fold in gently.

Spoon batter into 2 x 23 cm sandwich tins which have been greased, lined and floured. Bake in a preheated oven 180°C (350°F) for 25–30 minutes. Cool in tin for 5 minutes, then turn onto a wire rack.

Beat cream cheese and butter until smooth, gradually adding icing sugar and cocoa powder. Stir in brandy if desired. Sandwich the layers together with icing, ice the cake and sprinkle with shredded coconut to serve.

SAUCES

Tomato Sauce is a perennial favourite — turning meat and pasta meals into memorable creations. And the traditional sauce has so many variations: it can be spiced or seasoned or just left plain to allow the full flavour of the tomato to be enjoyed.
This chapter includes a range of tomato sauces plus the other sauces referred to in this book and dressings that may be served on the side or tossed with salads.

Fresh Tomato Sauce

2 kg tomatoes, cored, peeled
* and chopped*
2 cups vinegar
2 cups sugar
4 tablespoons salt
4 tablespoons black
* peppercorns*
4 tablespoons whole allspice
4 tablespoons crushed
* cinnamon sticks*
2 tablespoons mustard seeds
2 tablespoons whole cloves
1 teaspoon cayenne pepper

Put the tomatoes into a pan and cook gently until reduced to a pulp. Rub through a colander to remove the seeds.

Cook the strained pulp, vinegar and sugar gently for 2 hours or until thick, then season with salt. Tie the spices in a piece of muslin cloth and drop into the mixture. Gently boil the sauce, stirring occasionally, until the sauce reaches the desired consistency. Bottle and seal while hot.

Tomato and Lentil Sauce

2 tablespoons olive oil
1 onion, chopped
2 cloves garlic, crushed
1 cup red lentils, washed well
125 g mushrooms, sliced
410 g can tomato puree
2 teaspoons oregano
Parmesan cheese, to serve

Heat the olive oil in a large pan and fry the onion and garlic gently until soft and transparent. Add the lentils, mushrooms, tomato puree and oregano and mix well. Bring to the boil, then simmer for 20 minutes. Serve with spaghetti, sprinkling over Parmesan cheese on the top.

Serves 6

Tasty Tomato Sauce

15 g butter
3 tablespoons chopped onion
3 tablespoons chopped carrot
2 tablespoons chopped celery
1 tablespoon flour
1 tablespoon tomato paste
1½ cups vegetable stock
1 small clove garlic, peeled
salt and pepper, to taste
1 teaspoon sugar
1 bay leaf
pinch basil

Melt the butter in a saucepan, add the vegetables and fry gently until brown. Stir in the flour and cook to a sandy texture, allowing it to colour slightly. Mix in the tomato paste, then leave to cool.

Gradually add the boiling stock, stirring until it boils. Add the garlic, salt and pepper, sugar, bay leaf and basil. Simmer, uncovered, for 30–40 minutes, then taste and adjust the seasoning if necessary. Strain the sauce, reheating it before using.

Makes 2 cups

White Sauce

40 g butter
2 tablespoons flour
1 cup milk
salt and pepper, to taste

Melt the butter in a heavy based saucepan then stir in the flour. Stir for 1 minute, until the flour is foaming but not browned. Gradually whisk in the milk, stirring constantly. Bring to the boil and cook, stirring for a few minutes until sauce has thickened. Season with salt and pepper.

Home Style Tomato Sauce

Making your own Tomato Sauce leaves you with the satisfaction of knowing that the ingredients used are natural and wholesome without loads of added salt and sugar. If a smooth consistency is required, puree in a food processor or blender. Buy tomatoes when they are at their lowest price and ripest stage.

1 tablespoon oil
2 onions, chopped
5 ripe tomatoes, cored,
    peeled and chopped
2 tablespoons tomato paste
2 cloves garlic, crushed
1 tablespoon fresh oregano
    or 1 teaspoon dried
    oregano
1 tablespoon fresh basil or 1
    teaspoon dried basil
1 teaspoon sugar
salt and pepper, to taste

Heat the oil in a pan and gently fry the onions until golden brown. Add the remaining ingredients and simmer uncovered for 30 minutes or until thick. Pour the sauce into hot sterilised jars and seal with tight fitting lids. Store the sauce in the refrigerator.

Makes 1 litre

Tomato Puree

12 large, ripe tomatoes
1 cup diced green capsicum
    (pepper)
1½ cups chopped onion
1 stick celery, sliced
⅓ cup sugar
1 tablespoon salt

Core the tomatoes and cut them into thin wedges. Place all the ingredients into a pan, bring to a simmer over a moderate heat then cover and simmer for 35–40 minutes until the tomatoes have broken down to a pulp.

Spoon the mixture into an electric blender or food processor and process until smooth. This may be done in several batches. Pour the puree through a sieve back into the rinsed out pan and bring to the boil. Cook at a full rolling boil for 30 minutes, stirring occasionally.

Pour into hot, sterilised jars leaving a little space at the top of each jar. Screw the tops on the jars tightly. Bring a large pan of water to the boil. Carefully lower the filled jars into the pan and cook for 30 minutes. Lift from the pan and allow the jars to cool. Store in a cool, dark cupboard for up to 6 months. Refrigerate after opening.

Makes 3 litres

Spaghetti Sauce

500 g topside mince
1 onion, finely chopped
1 stalk celery, finely chopped
1 carrot, grated
1 clove garlic, crushed
410 g can peeled
    tomatoes, drained
3 tablespoons tomato paste
¾ cup red wine or beef stock
1½ teaspoons basil
salt and pepper, to taste

Combine all the ingredients in a large saucepan and bring slowly to the boil, stirring occasionally until well combined. Reduce the heat to medium and simmer uncovered for 1 hour. Pour the sauce over hot pasta, tossing well before serving.

Serves 6

Brown Sauce

60 g butter
1 onion, chopped
1 small carrot, peeled and
    chopped
½ stalk celery, chopped
1 tablespoon flour
2½ cups beef stock
1 tablespoon tomato paste
1 bouquet garni
¼ cup dry sherry
freshly ground black pepper,
    to taste

Melt the butter in a medium-sized, heavy-based saucepan. Add the vegetables and cook over a low heat until a rich golden colour, about 10 minutes. Add the flour and continue to cook, stirring until browned. Remove from heat and stir in the stock a little at a time. Stir in the tomato paste and add bouquet garni.

Return to heat and simmer for 10 minutes, stirring occasionally until sauce has thickened slightly and is a rich brown colour. Sieve to remove the vegetable pieces. Return to pan and flavour with sherry and pepper. Simmer for 5 minutes.

Makes 2 cups

BEVERAGES

The full-bodied flavour of the tomato acts as a perfect foil for alcohol and mixes and can be married with a surprisingly wide range of drinks and seasonings.

Try a tomato cocktail such as a Bloody Mary or Tipsy Tomato Cocktail for brunch. Tomatoes are equally delicious as a morning health drink or lunch time pick-me-up and can be mixed with other juices, like orange, or seasoned with herbs or spiced with chilli.

Whatever the drink, the tomatoes should be firm and ripe to ensure they have maximum flavour. Have the tomatoes at room temperature and make the drink just before serving, pouring it over ice cubes to add a slight chill. If making tomato juice to serve with alcohol, add it just before serving so any leftover juice can easily be used in a casserole or sauce.

Sherried Tomato Juice

¾ cup tomato juice
salt
pepper
dash Tabasco sauce
1 teaspoon dry sherry
Worcestershire sauce
lemon wedges, to garnish

Chill the tomato juice then season to taste with the salt, pepper and Tabasco sauce. Just before serving, stir in the sherry and a few drops of Worcestershire sauce to taste. Garnish with a thin wedge of lemon.

Makes 1 cup

Zesty Bloody Mary

2¼ cups tomato juice
1¼ cups vodka
1½ teaspoons Worcestershire
  sauce
½ teaspoon chilli sauce
¾ teaspoon celery salt
¼ teaspoon garlic powder
juice of 3 limes or lemons

Mix all the ingredients together, then pour over ice cubes into tall glasses.

Makes 3½ cups

Sherried Tomato Juice

Tipsy Tomato Cocktail

3½ cups tomato juice
½ cup claret
½ cup lemon juice
salt and pepper, to taste
⅛ teaspoon paprika
1 cup cream, whipped
1 teaspoon tomato paste

Mix the tomato juice with the claret and lemon juice, then season to taste with salt, pepper and paprika.

Stir the tomato paste into the cream. Serve the drink chilled and topped with the tomato cream. Garnish with a sprinkling of paprika.

Makes 6 cups

Citrus Tomato Mix

3–4 sprigs of mint
2 cups tomato juice
¾ cup orange juice
salt
sugar

Bruise the mint by crushing it gently between your fingers. Put it in a jug and pour over the tomato and orange juice. Season to taste with the salt and sugar. Chill thoroughly and leave for at least 1 hour to infuse before straining.

Makes 2¾ cups

Tomato Refresher

3 large tomatoes, cored,
*   peeled and chopped*
1 cucumber, peeled and
*   chopped*
1 stick celery, chopped

Combine all the ingredients in an electric blender or food processor and process until smooth. Pour into a glass jug and refrigerate. Serve cold with ice cubes.

Makes approximately 3 cups

Minted Tomato Juice

2 cups tomato juice
rind and juice of ½ lemon
1 teaspoon vinegar
1 teaspoon Worcestershire
*   sauce*
1 teaspoon finely chopped
*   mint*
salt, pepper and nutmeg, to
*   taste*

Combine all the ingredients together and chill thoroughly. Remove the lemon rind before serving.

Makes 2 cups

Yoghurt Tomato Mix

250 g tomatoes, cored,
*   peeled and chopped*
200 g carton yoghurt
¼ teaspoon Worcestershire
*   sauce*
¼ teaspoon lemon juice
paprika
mint leaves, for garnish

Puree the tomatoes in a food processor or blender. Mix the yoghurt, Worcestershire sauce and lemon juice, then season with a dash of paprika. Chill thoroughly and serve garnished with the mint leaves.

Makes approximately 2 cups

Hawaiian Tomato Drink

1½ cups tomato juice
½ cup unsweetened
*   pineapple juice*
2 teaspoons Worcestershire
*   sauce*
1 teaspoon lemon juice
salt
cayenne pepper
mint leaves, to garnish

Combine the tomato and pineapple juice with the sauce and lemon juice, then season to taste with the salt and cayenne pepper. Chill thoroughly and serve garnished with mint leaves.

Makes 2 cups

Herbed Tomato Juice

Served at breakfast, this juice will provide the energy to start the day.

1.5 kg tomatoes
½ cup water
1 onion, sliced
1 stick celery, sliced
4 sprigs basil or 1 teaspoon
*   dried basil*
3 sprigs of parsley
½ bay leaf
salt
paprika
dash Worcestershire sauce
lemon juice

Put the tomatoes into a pan with the water, onion, celery and herbs. Simmer until the tomatoes have broken up. Strain, then season to taste with salt, paprika, Worcestershire sauce and a dash of lemon juice. Pour into a glass jar and chill before serving.

Makes approximately 4 cups

PRESERVES AND JAMS

The homely sight of bottles and jars of preserves lining the pantry shelf is not as common today as it was a few generations ago. However, when they appear at fetes and market stalls, they disappear quickly and there never seems to be enough. Preserves are not at all difficult to make and can be very economical when a glut of tomatoes appears on the market stalls. So don't throw away those empty jars. Hoard them until tomatoes are cheap and plentiful and turn them into a delicious array of jams, pickles, chutneys and sauces that will last throughout the winter. Not only will your family enjoy them but they also make delightful and appreciated gifts.

Green Tomato Pickle

Wait until the frosts have taken the vines, and then use the remaining crop of green tomatoes for this pickle.

3 kg green tomatoes, cored
  and sliced
1 kg onions, sliced
½ cup salt
2 cups white vinegar
1½ cups sugar
3 whole cloves
1 tablespoon mustard
2 teaspoons cornflour

Layer the tomatoes alternately with the onions in a glass bowl, lightly sprinkling each layer with salt. Leave to stand overnight.

The next day, bring the vinegar, sugar and cloves to the boil. Make a paste of the mustard and cornflour and stir in a little vinegar to blend. Stir into the boiling vinegar. Wash and drain the tomatoes and onions and add to the vinegar. Cook for 1 hour, stirring occasionally until the pickle reaches the desired consistency.

Tomato Chutney

12 large ripe tomatoes, cored,
  peeled and chopped
6 medium apples, peeled,
  cored and chopped
6 red capsicums (peppers),
  seeded and chopped
4 green capsicums (peppers),
  seeded and chopped

4 large onions, chopped
1 red chilli, seeded and
  chopped
250 g seedless raisins
1 cup white vinegar
1 tablespoon sugar
2 teaspoons celery seeds
1 teaspoon salt

Mix all the ingredients together in a large pan and bring to the boil. Cook on low heat for 1 hour stirring occasionally until the chutney reaches the desired consistency. Bottle and seal while hot.

Tomato and Cucumber Pickle

3 kg green tomatoes, cored
  and sliced
1 kg cucumbers, peeled and
  thinly sliced
1 cup salt
2 red capsicums (peppers),
  seeded and finely chopped
3 cloves garlic, finely
  chopped

1 litre white vinegar
1½ cups sugar
1 tablespoon mustard
2 teaspoons turmeric
1 teaspoon ground allspice
1 teaspoon celery salt

Mix the tomatoes and cucumbers in a bowl, sprinkle evenly with salt and leave overnight.

The next day, wash and drain the tomato and cucumber mixture then combine with the remaining ingredients in a large saucepan. Cook gently for 1 hour, stirring occasionally, until the pickle reaches the desired consistency.

Pour into hot sterilised jars and seal. Store in a cool dark cupboard for up to 1 year. Refrigerate after opening.

Tomato Relish

3 kg tomatoes, cored, peeled
  and chopped
1 kg white onions, finely
  chopped
½ cup salt
2 cups vinegar
1½ cups sugar
2 tablespoons curry powder

1 tablespoon mustard
1 teaspoon ground mace
1 teaspoon ground cloves
1 teaspoon ground cinnamon
1 teaspoon ground ginger
1 teaspoon ground nutmeg
3 tablespoons cornflour

Mix the tomatoes and onions in a bowl, sprinkle with the salt and leave overnight

The next day, wash and drain the vegetables. Cover with the vinegar, then add the sugar and simmer, stirring constantly, until the sugar has dissolved. Mix the spices with the cornflour and blend with a little cold vinegar. Pour the paste into the relish and cook gently for 1 hour, stirring occasionally until the relish is of the desired consistency.

Mixed Chutney

Bottle the fruits of summer, and enjoy year round chutney.

1.5 kg apples, peeled, cored
   and chopped
1.5 kg tomatoes, cored,
   peeled and chopped
1.5 kg marrow, seeded and
   chopped
1 kg onions, chopped
250 g shallots (spring onions,
   scallions), chopped
250 g garlic, chopped

1 kg plums, stoned
1 kg sugar
½ cup salt
½ cup mustard seeds
1 tablespoon chopped green
   ginger
1 teaspoon chopped red
   chillies
1 teaspoon whole cloves

Simmer the apples in just enough water to cover until tender. Transfer to a large bowl and add the vegetables, fruit, sugar and salt. Leave to stand overnight.

The next day, tie the spices in a piece of muslin cloth and add it to the vegetable mixture. Simmer for 4 hours or until the chutney reaches the desired consistency.

Apple, Lemon and Green Tomato Chutney

12 black peppercorns
small knob green ginger,
   bruised
1 tablespoon dried red
   chillies
2 litres vinegar
500 g sugar
⅓ cup salt
2 kg green tomatoes, finely
   chopped

500 g marrow, seeded and
   finely chopped
500 g shallots (spring onions,
   scallions), finely chopped
1.5 kg apples, peeled, cored
   and finely chopped
500 g sultanas
juice 3 lemons

Tie the spices into a piece of muslin cloth and add them to the vinegar, sugar and salt. Boil gently for 50 minutes, stirring occasionally. Add the vegetables and fruit to the vinegar with the lemon juice and simmer for 3½–4 hours or until the chutney reaches the desired consistency. If necessary, add more vinegar. Bottle and seal while hot.

Hints for Jam Making

To prevent fruit from catching and burning on the bottom of the saucepan, rub a little butter inside the base of the pan before using.

To test jam for setting, spoon a little of the cooked jam onto a chilled saucer. Allow jam to cool then tilt the saucer and gently press the jam with your finger. If the jam wrinkles and feels quite thick, the jam has had sufficient cooking. If you have a sugar thermometer it will reach 105°C when the jam has reached its setting point.

To sterilise jars first wash clean jars in hot soapy water. Rinse with boiling water then turn the jars upside down on a clean dry tea towel. Using tongs place the jars onto a baking tray. Place in oven 160°C (325°F) for 15 minutes. Fill the hot jars with hot preserve.

1 Using a slotted spoon, carefully remove the froth which rises to the surface of the cooking jam

2 **Testing jam for setting point (Method 1)** Remove a small amount of hot jam with a spoon. Tilt the spoon, and if the jam comes away in large flake-like drops — not too runny — it has reached setting point.

3 **Testing jam for setting point (Method 2)** Spoon some hot jam onto a chilled saucer. Allow to cool, then gently push your finger into the jam. If it wrinkles on top the jam is set.

4 To sterilize glass jars wash in hot soapy water, drain and rinse with boiling water then place into oven preheated to 150°C (300°F) and leave for 15 minutes. Fill jars while still hot

Pineapple and Tomato Jam

1 large pineapple
1 kg tomatoes, cored and
   peeled
375 g sugar to each 500 g
   puree

Cut the pineapple in half and scoop out the flesh. Place into a large saucepan together with the tomatoes. Bring slowly to the simmer and cook until the pineapple is soft. Carefully weigh the mixture and return to the saucepan. Add the sugar according to weight. Return to heat and simmer, stirring until the sugar dissolves.

Bring to the boil and skim off any impurities that rise to the top. Boil for 1 hour or until the jam forms thick droplets when dropped from a metal spoon. Pour the jam into hot, sterilised jars and seal with tight-fitting lids.

Tomato Marmalade

4 oranges
1 lemon
2 kg tomatoes, cored, peeled
   and chopped
2 kg sugar

Finely slice the oranges and lemon, leaving the rind on. Add to the tomatoes and sugar and bring to the boil, stirring occasionally. Reduce the heat and cook gently for 1 hour or until the mixture forms thick droplets when dropped from a metal spoon. Pour into hot, sterilised jars and seal with tight fitting lids. Store for up to 2 years.

INDEX

Printed in Singapore